CANADIAN BATTLES

Canada's Role in Major World Conflicts

Norman Leach

FOLK LORE PUBLISHING

© 2009 by Folklore Publishing
First printed in 2009 10 9 8 7 6 5 4 3 2 1
Printed in Canada

All rights reserved. No part of this work covered by the copyrights hereon may be reproduced or used in any form or by any means—graphic, electronic or mechanical—without the prior written permission of the publisher, except for reviewers, who may quote brief passages. Any request for photocopying, recording, taping or storage on information retrieval systems of any part of this work shall be directed in writing to the publisher.

The Publisher: Folklore Publishing
Website: www.folklorepublishing.com

Library and Archives Canada Cataloguing in Publication

Leach, Norman, 1963–
  Canadian battles / by Norman Leach.

Includes bibliographical references.

ISBN 978-1-894864-78-7

  1. Battles—Canada—History. 2. Canada—History, Military. I. Title.

FC226.L42 2009   971   C2009-900202-7

Project Director: Faye Boer
Project Editor: Paul Deans
Cover Image: AR2008-J011-181; National Defence; www.combatcamera.forces.ca.
Reproduced with permission of the Minister of Public Works and Government Services. 2009.
Back Cover Image: © Nantela/Dreamstime.com The Great War.

We acknowledge the support of the Alberta Foundation for the Arts for our publishing program.

We acknowledge the financial support of the Government of Canada through the Book Publishing Industry Development Program (BPIDP) for our publishing activities.

   Canadian Patrimoine
Heritage canadien

PC:1

Dedication

Without the support and patience of many people, a book such as this would never be completed. In my case, I have three very supportive, patient and loving muses: my wife Maritza and my daughters Stephanie and Chelsea. I owe this book to them.

Contents

WORLD WAR II

MODERN-ERA BATTLES

NOTES ON SOURCES

Acknowledgements

A BOOK OF ANY TYPE, BUT ESPECIALLY one about military history, needs three things: a publisher who has the courage to invest in a book that covers an important subject, a writer who does justice to the topic and an editor who brings it all together—and to life.

This book benefited from just such a publisher in Faye Boer, who recognized that Canadians need to know more about their own history. It also benefited from a great editor, Paul Deans. Paul held my feet to the fire, and by doing so made this book so much the better. A hearty "thank you" to both of them.

I only hope my writing does the two of them justice and lives up to their trust in me.

Introduction

FOR THE PAST 50 YEARS, PEACEKEEPING has defined Canada's military role in the world. To Canadians born after 1960, the only view they have of Canadian soldiers is of blue-beret-wearing peacekeepers.

However, Canada has a long and varied military past. In fact, our country was defined in a battle—on the Plains of Abraham during the Seven Years' War between the French and the British. As Canada became something more than a colony but still less than a free and independent county, she faced an external threat during the War of 1812 and internal rebellion in 1837. Each of these conflicts tempered the country and its citizens, and helped grow the belief in the value of an armed militia of citizen soldiers.

In 1856, at the height of the Crimean War, Britain was in desperate need of trained and battle-ready troops. She looked to her colony in North America and realized that the British troops defending Canada could be better used in the Crimea. Britain ordered the garrisons to withdraw, leaving the Canadians responsible for their own defence. It was this departure (among other events) that encouraged Canada to declare herself independent in 1867.

With independence, Canada started to chart her own military and foreign policy, though ties with Great Britain remained strong for the rest of the 19th century. These ties encouraged the Fenians to attack Canada in 1866 and 1870 with the hope of drawing

Britain back into North America and away from the fight for independence in Ireland.

While the Fenians were unsuccessful, it was only 15 years later that the fledgling country was again threatened. In 1885 Louis Riel and a combined force of Métis and Native fighters rebelled against Canadian rule in what is now Saskatchewan. With a stated goal of independence and possible amalgamation with the United States, Riel threatened the very existence of a cross-continental Canada. The victory of Canadian militia over the rebels spurred settlement and development in the lands west of Ontario. Canada was fast becoming a country in control of all of her territory from coast to coast.

The end of the 19th century saw Canada, for the first time, fully support Britain in an overseas expedition. When war broke out between the British and the Boers in South Africa, Canada answered the call and sent troops in support of Imperial interests. Canadian infantry and cavalry units distinguished themselves on the field of battle and earned a reputation as tough and disciplined troops. It was a distinction that followed Canadians soldiers to the battlefields of France when World War I broke out in August 1914. Canada sent troops to fight and die in places such as Vimy Ridge, Passchendaele and Amiens.

Canadian soldiers fought together as a unit for the first time at the Battle of Vimy Ridge, while at Passchendaele, Canadians were commanded for the first time by a Canadian General. At Amiens, the Canadians led the Allied forces forward. And in another first, during the little-known Siberian campaign at the end of the war, a Canadian general led British troops in the field. The former colony in North American had come a long way.

After World War I, Canada and her armed forces were full-fledged members of the community of nations. No longer just an afterthought in British foreign policy, Canada was consulted and her views heard. She had earned her place at the international table through the blood of her soldiers.

In 1939, when Hitler's Nazis invaded Poland and plunged the world into yet another war, Canadian soldiers were once more on the front lines. Soldiers, sailors and airmen from Canada distinguished themselves during the next six years as they participated in every major action and battle in the European theatre of operations. Combat in places with names like Dieppe, Normandy and Ortona cemented Canada's place in military history.

With the memories of World War II still fresh, Canada started the process of disarming and returning her men to their civilian jobs. All Canadians hoped that they had earned a long period of uninterrupted peace. It was not to be. By the end of World War II old alliances were broken, new powers had come to the fore and fresh conflicts raged.

In Korea the United Nations, supported by troops from around the world (including Canadians), struggled to bring order to a chaotic situation. Just as the Korean conflict ended, Egypt's President Nasser dragged the world to the edge of nuclear war when he took over the Suez Canal Zone and prompted a conflict with Britain and France. Again the UN was challenged to find a way to get the combatants to back down.

A Canadian, Lester B. Pearson, championed the idea of a United Nations Peacekeeping Force that defined Canada's international role in a new way. Neutral UN troops, loaned by participating governments to the mission, inserted themselves between the combatants to enforce a sometimes tenuous peace. Canada was earning a new place of influence in the world.

Since its participation in Egypt, Canada has served in every peacekeeping mission the United Nations has undertaken. Canadians have been on the ground in Cyprus, the Golan Heights, and Bosnia. These are the missions that Canadians have come to expect from our modern-day soldiers, sailors and airmen.

Recently, with its participation in the UN-mandated and NATO-led effort to assist the people of Afghanistan, Canada has returned to a well-known role. Canadian soldiers are again in a war, fighting beside international allies, in an effort to stop tyranny and to bring a better life to the average Afghan citizen.

Yes, Canada has a military tradition. It is a long and proud one, and one that has seen Canadian soldiers, sailors and airmen sacrifice their lives for their country and its place in the world. Theirs is a sacrifice we must not forget and is a story worth telling.

CANADIAN BATTLES

The Beginnings
of Canada

CHAPTER ONE

The Plains of Abraham
September 1759

To the British and French fighting the Seven Years' War in Europe, North America seemed a long way off. Yet on September 12, 1759, Québec City in New France became the focus of the two European rivals. The Battle of the Plains of Abraham pitted the British Army and Navy against the French Army on a plateau just outside Québec City. The battle, involving only 10,000 troops, helped bring an end to the French and Indian War and laid the groundwork for a new country—Canada—in North America.

In 1759, Québec was a fortified city defended by French General Louis-Joseph de Montcalm. Attacking the city was British General James Wolfe. Throughout the summer Wolfe besieged Québec City, trying to force Montcalm to either fight or surrender. It had not gone well for the British.

Wolfe wanted to draw Montcalm into a battle that, he hoped, would end the French presence in North America. Montcalm refused to face Wolfe in an open battle and continued to reinforce his positions in the city. Wolfe and many of his men were sick and confined to their beds. As each day went by, the British Army grew weaker, and Wolfe knew it. In the face of

ever-decreasing morale in the ranks, Wolfe realized
that he had to fight by the end of September, or his
army might not survive the cold Canadian winter.

Finally, Wolfe and his officers devised a plan to
force Montcalm out of Québec City and into a battle.
Wolfe considered a number of options but finally settled on a landing on the North Shore of the St. Lawrence River above Québec City. Counting on surprise,
he planned an assault that would see a small group of
men climb the cliff, overpower the battery and open a
path for the 4400 British soldiers waiting below—all
under the cover of darkness.

Despite warnings from his commanders, Montcalm
did not believe that Wolfe could land a substantial
number of men on shore without being detected.
Wolfe, in an effort to disguise his real intentions, sent
landing craft full of men up and down the river for
days before the actual planned landings. On the night
of September 12, Wolfe ordered his men to put in at
L'Ánse-au-Foulon, a cove southwest of Québec City.
Protected by a battery of French guns perched atop a
50-metre cliff, L'Ánse-au-Foulon appeared to be the
last place for a British amphibious landing.

French Brigadier Bougainville, responsible for
defending the area between Cap Diamant and Cap
Rouge, was away from the area that day and did not
see the British force as it landed. The French did notice
a large number of ships moving but, expecting a
French supply convoy, assumed the ships were their
own and did not raise an alarm. However, French

sentries posted on the riverbank did see the boats coming ashore and raised a challenge. A French-speaking British officer responded fluently that all was well and the sentries should go back to their business. The British troops landed unopposed.

A group of volunteers with fixed bayonets scrambled up the cliffs and at the top captured the small group of French sentries. Behind the volunteers came three companies of British regulars. As they surveyed the plateau in front of them, the British were surprised to find the ground undefended except for a small camp of soldiers, who were quickly overpowered. By dawn the British were firmly established on the Plains of Abraham.

In the confusion, a French sentry was able to escape capture and make his way to Montcalm's headquarters. Demanding he be allowed to see Montcalm, the runner was declared completely mad by one of the General's aides who, after sending the man away, calmly returned to his bed. Montcalm soon realized that the runner had indeed been telling the truth. He quickly made up his mind to attack. Speaking to an artillery officer, Montcalm said: "We cannot avoid action; the enemy is entrenching, he already has two pieces of cannon. If we give him time to establish himself, we shall never be able to attack him with the troops we have."

In fact, had Montcalm simply waited, the British would have been cut off by French reinforcements and forced to withdraw down the cliff face—this time under fire. Instead, Montcalm advanced on the British positions. In total, Montcalm had 13,390 regular troops, Troupes de la Marine and militia as well as 200 cavalry, 200 artillery (including the guns of Québec), 300 Native warriors and 140 Acadian volunteers, but most of the French forces never saw action.

On the morning of September 13, Wolfe ordered his 4400 men to form a shallow horseshoe that backed against the river and spread out across the Plains. A bluff along the St. Lawrence River anchored the right end of the line, and a bluff and thick wood above the St. Charles River anchored the left. To conserve manpower and extend his lines, Wolfe ordered the men to form just two ranks rather than the more conventional three.

While the regular French forces were approaching from Beauport and Québec City, the Canadian militia and Native sharpshooters, hiding in the trees and shrubs, opened fire on the British. A spirited engagement followed, with the militia falling back to a bridge on the St. Charles River. They remained at the bridge for the rest of the battle, neither gathering more territory nor ceding any.

The British consolidated their positions in house-to-house fighting. Many of the residents burned their own homes rather than see them fall into enemy hands. The burning homes created a smokescreen that obscured the size and depth of the British left flank. To avoid breathing the acrid air, Wolfe ordered his men to lie down in the high grass, which had the added benefit of further hiding the size of his force from the advancing French.

Montcalm, mounted on his charger, was now moving among the French troops on the battlefield and personally took control of the French side. He assessed the situation and decided that if Wolfe was to be defeated, it was necessary to attack immediately with the 4400 men he had from Québec City and not wait for reinforcements from Beauport. Montcalm quickly ordered his men to form columns and prepare for an assault. At 10:00 AM Montcalm raised his sword above his head and ordered a general advance on the British line.

Even as the French marched forward, the British solders realized that their general had chosen the battlefield well. While Montcalm occupied the higher ground, a slight rise at the centre of the battlefield meant that the centre of Montcalm's column had to veer slightly to the left to avoid the rise, weakening the right-hand side of the attack. As the right side thinned, fewer and fewer French soldiers were in place to attack the British left flank.

Wolfe and his men were ready and waiting for the enemy. Wolfe's strategy called for his men to hold their fire until the French were only 20 metres away before opening fire. It took well-trained and steady troops to hold while the enemy approached to point-blank range. Wolfe also ordered his men to put two balls into each of their muskets, meaning that a single volley would be twice as deadly.

Finally, with the French almost close enough to touch, the British fired. The French troops were shaken, and their ranks started to break up in confusion. The British—still in formation—reloaded, took a few steps forward and fired again. For the French it was too much. Their nerve broken, they bolted in retreat though a few continued fighting.

Wolfe, nursing a wounded wrist but still wanting to see the battle unfold, moved to a small knoll to gain a better vantage point. There, as he watched his troops advance, Wolfe was struck by a bullet in the stomach and another in the chest. As he lay dying, British troops began a disorganized pursuit of the retreating French soldiers. Montcalm, still mounted and leading his men, was hit by bullets in both the abdomen and thigh. He made it back to Québec City but died the next day.

The Battle of the Plains of Abraham claimed 644 French and 658 British casualties. Following tradition, the French governor, Pierre François de Rigaud, Marquis de Vaudreuil-Cavagnal, replaced Montcalm and blamed the loss on his predecessor. He immediately abandoned the city and the Beauport shore, marched west and left Québec under the command of Jean-Baptiste-Nicolas-Roch de Ramezay.

On September 18 the British ended their siege of Québec City when de Ramezay, Viscount George Townshend (who became the British commander at Wolfe's death) and Admiral Charles Saunders signed the Articles of Capitulation of Québec. The city was now completely in British control. What was left of the French forces gathered on the Jacques-Cartier River west of the city to await further instructions.

As winter closed in, the British Navy left the St. Lawrence River so as not to be trapped in the ice. In the spring of 1760, Vaudreuil headed back to Québec City—with 7000 troops. On April 28, 1760, British and French forces clashed west of the city at the Battle of St. Foy. This time the French were victorious, but the British were able to withdraw inside Québec City's fortifications and wait for the arrival of the British Navy. In mid-May, once the river ice had melted, the Navy arrived and the siege was lifted.

It took a few more months, but on September 8, 1760, the French finally conceded that the British had been victorious. They relinquished possession of Montréal, and the land that ultimately became Canada was passed to the British. The Treaty of Paris, signed in 1763, made it official: New France belonged to Great Britain. 1763

CHAPTER TWO

Restigouche
July 1760

IN THE SPRING OF 1759, THE BRITISH NAVY was blockading the French-controlled cities of Québec and Montréal. Despite the heavy naval presence, a French supply convoy successfully ran the blockade and delivered its goods to both cities. But it was too little too late. That autumn, Québec City fell to the British, and the French Governor Pierre François de Rigaud, Marquis de Vaudreuil-Cavagnal was forced to withdraw.

However, Vaudreuil was not yet ready to surrender. On September 25 he ordered the 30-gun frigate *Le Machault* and four merchant vessels to run the gauntlet yet again and head for France, carrying an urgent request for 4000 troops, food, ammunition and clothing so that he could re-engage the British. The ships made it to France, and Vaudreuil's request was presented to King Louis XV.

The King responded, but not with everything that Vaudreuil had asked for. His Majesty sent five cargo ships under the protection of the *Le Machault* back to New France, laden with tons of supplies but with only 400 veterans of Louisbourg and Québec, not the 4000 soldiers requested. France was nearing her limit in the Seven Years' War with England, and these were all the soldiers the King could spare.

From the very beginning the relief mission was in danger. The small convoy had barely headed out to sea when two British warships were spotted on the horizon. Unfortunately for the French ships, they were seen too. The captain of the *Le Machault*, Lieutenant François La Giraudais, ordered the convoy to scatter, hoping that in the confusion, they could all get away. However, only two ships rejoined the *Le Machault*—the others were never seen again.

On May 15 the three ships were ready to enter the St. Lawrence when the *La Machault* captured a British warship. Papers on the British vessel told the French that five British ships of the line, three frigates and three corvettes, were ahead, awaiting anyone trying to run the blockade. The French ships headed for the Baie des Chaleurs (below the Gaspé Peninsula) to hide from the British fleet, while a courier was put ashore to rendezvous with Governor Vaudreuil. On the way, the *Le Machault* captured four British merchant ships that the French crews quickly manned and added to their growing fleet.

As the French entered Baie des Chaleurs on May 17, the *Le Machault* captured yet another British merchant. Two days later, La Giraudais ordered his convoy up the Restigouche River and dropped anchor at what became known as Battery Point. La Giraudais knew they had been lucky so far. With so many British warships in the area, it would not be long until word got back to the British commanders that the English merchantmen were missing.

Even as La Giraudais reinforced his position by building a battery on shore and sending patrol boats up and down the river, the British heard rumours about the French fleet. Local Natives told the captain of a British patrol vessel that strange ships were on the Restigouche River. On June 18 the HMS *Fame* (commanded by Captain John Byron), accompanied by the ships of the line HMS *Dorsetshire* and HMS *Achilles* and the frigates *Repulse* and *Scarborough*, headed out to investigate.

Hit by a storm, the squadron was unable to stay in contact, and Byron decided to head to the Restigouche on his own, hoping the other ships would catch up. Almost immediately the *Fame* came upon a French schooner and quickly overtook her. The French captain beached his boat at Magouacha Point, abandoned the ship and headed inland to rejoin La Giraudais and the others.

Captain Byron and a small crew rowed up the river in a longboat. He quickly returned to the *Fame* when he realized that the French were fortifying the point that controlled the mouth of the Restigouche with four twelve-pound cannons and one six-pound cannon. But as Byron sailed the *Fame* toward the French position, she ran aground on a sandbar 14 kilometres short of her target.

As Byron and his crew worked to free the *Fame*, La Giraudais and his men further strengthened their position. He ordered a number of the captured British merchantmen scuttled in a line across the river, which would make it very difficult for the British ships to pass the point—especially under fire from the French position.

By this time the other British warships had rejoined the *Fame*, and together they advanced on Battery Point. The British ships continually ran aground on sandbars and had to be refloated each time. Meanwhile, La Giraudais ordered the French fleet as far up the Restigouche as possible, leaving Captain de la Valliere, 60 soldiers and 100 Acadians to man the battery of guns.

On June 27 both sides were ready for battle. The British warships were lined up just outside the line of sunken merchantmen. First Lieutenant Donat La Garde opened fire, and for the rest of the day the warships and battery exchanged shot for shot. As darkness fell, Byron ordered the ships to fall back. For the next five days cannon fire echoed across the Restigouche with neither side gaining an advantage.

When the frontal attack proved futile, Byron gradually worked the *Fame* into the south channel of the river and opened fire from behind the battery. With the French guns unable to return the *Fame*'s fire, La Garde realized the battle was lost, spiked his guns and retreated. Byron destroyed the battery and ordered the village of Restigouche burned to the ground.

As the French retreated upriver, the British slowly followed. The larger British ship kept hanging up on sandbars, and finally the *Fame* could go no farther. However, the smaller *Repulse* and *Scarborough* continued the pursuit. La Giraudais was able to stay ahead of his pursuers by using local Acadians as pilots—men who knew the river far better than the British.

As the Restigouche River narrowed between Campbellton and Cross Point, and with a sustained lead on his pursuers, La Giraudais took the time to establish a new battery on each side of the river. He then positioned the *Le Machault* so its 10 twelve-pound cannons and one six-pounder could support the batteries. He sank the final captured British schooner to establish a defensive line and then waited for the British to come to him.

Byron, constrained by the narrowing river, ordered the French schooner (beached earlier in the battle and recovered by the British) to move forward and destroy the south-shore battery. But armed with only four six-pounders and 50 men, the small ship was unable to have any effect against the battery. Desperate to silence the battery, Byron ordered the *Repulse* and *Scarborough* to lower their boats. Under heavy gunfire, the British sailors towed the frigates through the shallow water toward the French position. Once the ships were within range, their broadsides wreaked havoc on the battery, and it was soon out of commission.

The next morning, July 3, Byron ordered the frigates pulled within range of the *La Machault* and opened fire. The French ships returned fire, hitting the *Repulse* multiple times. The *Repulse* settled to the bottom of the river, but the water was so shallow her crew was able to quickly patch her hull and pump out the water. Soon her guns were again pounding the French warships.

The battle raged for hours, but the end was inevitable. Despite the courage of the French crews, their ships eventually ran out of powder. Unable to fire, the ships were floating targets for the British gun crews. Looking around, La Giraudais realized the merchant ship *Bienfaisant* was in flames, and the *Marquis de Malauze* was out of commission. La Giraudais reluctantly ordered his crew to abandon the *La Machault* and, in a final act of defiance, ordered her burned. He then removed the cannons from the *Marquis* and left it abandoned.

Once on shore, La Giraudais organized his men to defend the stores that had been removed from the ships. He was determined, if at all possible, to complete his mission of resupplying Québec and Montréal. Byron was just as determined to destroy the supplies. He ordered the recovered schooner, 17 boats and 400 men to attack the French position. Bypassing the north-shore battery, the British soon forced the French to destroy another four ships to keep them out of British hands. As night fell it was clear the French were defeated, and Byron ordered his men back to their ships. The French fleet was destroyed at a cost of only 24 British casualties. The battle appeared to be over.

The next morning Byron recognized his small fleet was not yet safe. The French warships were out of commission, but the north-shore battery commanded by First Lieutenant Reboul was still very much in action, and the French were determined to not let the British escape. As the ships moved toward the battery, the British realized English prisoners were still on the abandoned *Marquis*. Byron ordered his warships to keep up a constant stream of fire while longboats were sent to rescue his men. Finally the British ships broke through and passed the battery. By July 8, the battle was over.

La Giraudais rebuilt his defences and constructed supply depots to protect the goods he had managed to salvage from his merchant fleet. Unfortunately for him, his efforts weren't enough. Although La Giraudais managed to hold out against a British fleet for 17 days along 24 kilometres of river, his eventual defeat meant France was finished in America. With Britain in control on both water and land, France had no option but to quit North America. On August 10, 1760, La Giraudais headed for France, with the last dispatches from Quebec's governor Vaudreuil in his possession. Less than one month later, the French officially surrendered.

CANADIAN BATTLES

The War
of 1812

CHAPTER THREE

Beaver Dams
June 1813

ON MAY 25, 1813, THE AMERICANS defeated the British at the Battle of Fort George. With the Stars and Stripes flying above the fort, which was situated on the western bank of the Niagara River, the Americans gave chase to the defeated British. The poorly organized pursuit ended in early June when the U.S. forces were defeated at the Battle of Stoney Creek. The Americans then retired to the protection of Fort George to plan their next move.

With the Americans ensconced in the fort, the British reoccupied positions at Twelve Mile Creek and Beaver Dams. The American commander, Brigadier General John Parker Boyd, hoping to relieve the constant harassment from the Canadian militia and their Native allies, ordered Colonel Charles Boerstler to attack Beaver Dams. His command consisted of detachments of the 6th, 13th and 23rd U.S. Infantry, the whole of the 14th Infantry, a company of artillery with two six-pounder field guns, 20 United States Dragoons and 40 mounted New York Militia volunteers. On the night of June 22, after a day of driving rain, Boerstler's force quietly left the safety of Fort George.

Led by Cyrenius Chapin, a guide from Buffalo, the Americans headed for the nearby village of Queenston and the hamlet of Saint David's. It soon became clear to all involved that Chapin was incompetent and had no knowledge of the territory into which the force was heading. They travelled 11 kilometres and arrived in Queenston at midnight, but in the process managed to broadcast their presence to the surrounding area.

Boerstler ordered his officers and men to seek refuge for the rest of the night in the various homes, barns and buildings in Queenston. Some of the officers found themselves in the home of Canadian Captain James Secord, who had been wounded at the Battle of Queenston Heights (in October 1812) and was no longer able to walk without assistance.

Underestimating Secord because of his handicap, the American officers openly discussed their plans for the next day in front of him and his wife Laura. Waking early the next morning, Laura slipped out of the house and started for Beaver Dams. She was stopped at the edge of Queenston by American sentries, but she convinced the soldiers that she had a cow to milk, and it would be on their heads if the cow became ill. The Americans allowed Laura to pass.

Moving quickly through the woods, Secord covered 30 kilometres, collapsing as she reached a Mohawk village friendly to the British and militia forces. The journey took her 18 hours. Braving the wilds of the thick woods, she had risked capture and

possible execution by either the Americans or by
Native forces opposed to the British. After giving her
a few minutes to recover, the warriors led her to
Lieutenant James Fitzgibbon, the officer commanding the Beaver Dams outpost.

Fitzgibbon immediately acted on Secord's information. He placed 300 Kahnawake Mohawks (under
the command of Captain Dominique Ducharme) on
one side of the road he knew the Americans would
use to approach his position, while on the other side,
hidden in the thick woods, were 100 Mohawks under
the command of Captain William Johnson Kerr.
Fitzgibbon, considered a higher rank than the two
captains because he was commanding British troops,
held back 46 men of the 49th Regiment of Foot. With
his trap set two kilometres east of his outpost,
Fitzgibbon waited for the Americans to come to him.
He did not have long to wait.

Late on the morning of June 24, Boerstler ordered
his men toward Beaver Dams. As the Americans
approached Fitzgibbon's position, the U.S. scouts
realized they were being observed by a large number
of Mohawks and that the warriors were closing in on
their flanks. Boerstler discounted the threat, believing he could get through the woods and out onto the
open plain in front of Beaver Dams. He knew that
once on the plain, his cannon would give him an
advantage over his lightly armed opponents.

The Mohawks chose not to engage in a frontal
attack but instead harassed the Americans with sniper

fire from behind cover. Almost immediately a musket ball hit Boerstler. Severely wounded, he was forced to command his troops from the back of a supply wagon.

The Americans tried to return fire, but they could not see any real targets in the thick forest that surrounded them. Unable to find an enemy to engage, and with their leader wounded, the American's morale began slipping as the soldiers feared they might be massacred. Fitzgibbon, recognizing that a massacre really was possible, approached the Americans carrying a flag of truce.

Speaking to Boerstler, Fitzgibbon explained that the Canadians had a vastly larger force (not true— the forces were about even). He added that the Mohawks were not fully under his control, so he was not sure what the result might be if the Americans did not surrender. When Fitzgibbon pointed out that the Mohawks had a reputation for killing all their enemies—even the wounded—and taking scalps, Boerstler capitulated and surrendered his 484 men. In 1818 Fitzgibbon wrote to Captain Kerr.

With respect to the affair with Captain (sic) Boerstler, not a shot was fired on our side by any but the Indians. They beat the American detachment into a state of terror, and the only share I claim is taking advantage of a favourable moment to offer them protection from the tomahawk and scalping knife. The Indian Department did the rest.

When asked why he had not demanded the American surrender, as he was the officer leading the fighting forces, Captain Ducharme claimed that he spoke no English, since he was a French Canadian by birth and had spent most of his life among the Indians. Local legend later described the Battle of Beaver Dams as one where: "The Kahnawake got the victory, the Mohawks got the plunder and Fitzgibbon got the credit."

The number of casualties at the Battle of Beaver Dams is debatable. The Mohawks reported five chiefs and warriors killed and 20 wounded, though Ducharme stated that 15 were killed and 25 wounded. The Americans admitted to 100 casualties and claimed that their dead had been scalped, though no proof of the mutilations was ever provided.

Boerstler was allowed to write to Major General Henry Dearborn, commander of the northern frontier from Niagara to the Atlantic coast, to explain what had happened during the battle. He recognized that there was some hope he would be exchanged for British prisoners of war and concluded his letter with signing "Your distressed humble servant," and then adding "I presume my destination will be Quebec, I beg that I may be exchanged as soon as possible."

In Washington, the American government was both disappointed and angry at the defeat at Beaver Dams. Calls were soon heard for Dearborn's removal, with men like Congressman Charles Ingersoll describing the actions at Beaver Dams as: "...(the) climax of continual mismanagement and misfortune."

Boerstler had hoped that a quick victory at Beaver Dams would bolster his men's morale and lead to more victories. In fact, the loss made the Americans ineffective as a fighting force as the fort's commander refused to authorize patrols farther than a half kilometre from his front door.

The final blow to the Americans came on July 8, when men from the 8th Kings Regiment and some Provincial Dragoons, along with a party of Mohawks led by Chief John Norton, were sent to retrieve a chest of medicines. The chest had been buried at Ball's Farm near Two Mile Creek when the British had evacuated Fort George.

The Americans, sensing the opportunity for a quick victory when pickets spotted the advancing forces, sent Lieutenant Joseph Eldridge and men from the 13th U.S. Infantry to engage the British. Instead, the Mohawks spotted the Americans, a hasty ambush was put in place, and the Americans suffered 28 killed when the combined British and Mohawk forces sprang the trap.

Within the context of the War of 1812, the Battle of Beaver Dams was a very minor clash. But for Canadians, it is part of Canada's national heritage because of the heroism of Laura Secord. Born in Massachusetts, Secord was a Loyalist whose family moved to Canada after the American Revolution. Her effort to notify Fitzgibbon of the American presence in Queenston, and the danger to the outpost at Beaver Dams, has become legend.

In 1827, writing of the incident, Fitzgibbon supported Secord's version of events:

I do hereby Certify that on the 22d. day of June 1813, Mrs. Secord, Wife of James Secord, Esqr. then of St. David's, came to me at the Beaver Dam after Sun Set, having come from her house at St. David's by a circuitous route a distance of twelve miles, and informed me that her Husband had learnt from an American officer the preceding night that a Detachment from the American Army then in Fort George would be sent out on the following morning (the 23d.) for the purpose of Surprising and capturing a Detachment of the 49th Regt. then at Beaver Dam under my Command. In Consequence of this information, I placed the Indians under Norton together with my own Detachment in a Situation to intercept the American Detachment and we occupied it during the night of the 22d. - but the Enemy did not come until the morning of the 24th when his Detachment was captured. Colonel Boerstler, their commander, in a conversation with me confirmed fully the information communicated to me by Mrs. Secord and accounted for the attempt not having been made on the 23rd. as at first intended.

Some historians, pointing out that the dates in Fitzgibbon's account do not match the ones in other accounts of the Secord story, believe that she may not have actually travelled 30 kilometres through the woods, and that it was the scouts attached to the Mohawk force who sounded the warning. This discrepancy is unlikely to be resolved, but the story of Laura Secord at the Battle of Beaver Dams will continue to inspire Canadians.

CHAPTER FOUR

Lake Erie
September 1813

WHEN WAR WAS DECLARED BETWEEN the United States and Great Britain in 1812, Canada was immediately involved. With the American's only warship on Lake Erie (the brig *Adams*) pinned down in Detroit, the British Navy quickly established control of the lake. When Detroit fell, the British added the unfinished *Adams* to their fleet and renamed her the HMS *Detroit*.

The Americans knew that if they were going to defeat the British, they needed to establish a naval force on Lake Erie. In March 1813, Master Commandant Oliver Hazard Perry was ordered to Presque Isle to take command of two new corvettes that were being built on the direct orders of William Jones, the Secretary of the Navy.

Perry quickly arranged the defences on Presque Isle and then headed to Lake Ontario to meet with Commodore Isaac Chauncey. While there, Perry was pressed into service at the Battle of Fort George where, on May 27, he commanded the American force of schooners and gunboats. At the end of May, on his way back to Lake Erie, Perry was ordered to Black Rock to take possession of the American vessels that the British released when they abandoned Fort Erie.

He then returned to Presque Isle with the ships literally in tow.

On the other side, Commander Robert Heriot Barclay took control of the British squadron. His was a modest command. Despite repeated requests to Commodore James L. Yeo, Barclay had only seven British seaman, 108 officers and men of the Provincial Marine, 54 men of the Royal Newfoundland Fencibles and 106 soldiers from the 41st Foot.

On July 20, Yeo ordered Barclay onto Lake Erie to establish a blockade of Presque Isle. Even though the British blockade stopped the flow of ships and supplies to the Americans, Perry continued to build up his squadron. But even as his ships neared completion, manpower remained a problem. Perry reported that he had only 120 men fit for duty.

Despite his orders to keep the Americans bottled up, Barclay was forced to abandon the blockade when his supplies ran short and a storm rolled in. Perry seized the opportunity to put his ships into deeper water and sailed out of port. Reprovisioned, Barclay returned to Presque Isle four days later to find Perry's squadron afloat and apparently ready for a fight. As the Americans pulled their ships into a line, seemingly ready to fire, Barclay backed down. He had no way of knowing that he had been bluffed; the American brigs were not yet ready for a real battle.

Perry sailed for Sandusky, Ohio, where he rendez-voused with Major General William Henry Harrison and took aboard a number of volunteers. He was now ready for a fight. Barclay twice saw Perry's ships off Amherstburg but felt that his best course of action was to wait for the HMS *Detroit* to be completed before engaging the Americans. However, when Perry established a blockade and pinned the British in Amherstburg for more than five weeks, Barclay knew he had no choice. Running low on provisions, he had to face a fight with the American squadron.

Early in the morning of September 10, 1813, Barclay headed his ships directly toward the Americans at Put-in-Bay. Perry responded by quickly ordering his ships to get under sail. The light wind meant that the U.S. brigs *Lawrence* and *Niagara* struggled to move quickly into firing range. Armed only with short-range carronades, the U.S. brigs came under devastating fire from the HMS *Detroit,* which possessed long guns with greater range. For 20 minutes the *Lawrence* endured a severe pounding, and even when she got within cannonade range, her inexperienced gunners overloaded the guns and severely limited their effectiveness.

The *Niagara*, commanded by Captain Jesse D. Elliott, followed behind the *Lawrence* but was not able to get into carronade range. Later, Perry and Elliot openly feuded about Elliot's inaction at the battle, which Elliot defended by saying that he had been blocked by the USS *Caledonia* and was not able to fire.

The British did not escape unscathed. On the *Queen Charlotte*, Commander Robert Finnis and his First Lieutenant were killed by American fire. Taking control, Lieutenant Irvine of the Provincial Marine recognized that the *Niagara* and the American gunboats had moved out of range, so he directed his fire on the *Lawrence.*

On the *Lawrence,* the crew knew the ship was finished. The gunboats tried to relieve the pressure on her by engaging the British warships, but the *Lawrence* was reduced to a wreck with 80 percent of her crew dead and wounded. Perry made the decision to transfer his flag to the *Niagara* just as the last gun on the *Lawrence* was put out of commission by British cannon fire. Perry lowered his personal pennant (with the words "Don't Give Up the Ship" emblazoned on it), boarded a longboat and was rowed a kilometre to the *Niagara.* As he left, the commander of the *Lawrence* surrendered her to the British.

As the *Lawrence* lowered her flag, the firing briefly died away. Almost immediately the HMS *Detroit* collided with the *Queen Charlotte,* and their rigging became hopelessly tangled. It didn't help that almost every officer on both ships was either killed or wounded. Many of the smaller British vessels near these two ships were damaged and drifting aimlessly. Yet Barclay believed the Americans were finished and would retreat from battle.

Perry had other plans. Now on board the *Niagara,* he ordered Elliot to direct the gunboats back into the fray while he personally steered the *Niagara* at Barclay's damaged squadron and positioned the American ship to continue firing broadsides. As the

crews of the HMS *Detroit* and *Queen Charlotte* freed
their ships, Barclay was severely wounded by one of
the *Niagara*'s broadsides. As he lay bleeding on the
deck, the *Niagara* and the American schooners
surrounded what was left of the British squadron,
forcing the *Detroit* and *Queen Charlotte* to surrender.
The remaining British ships made a run for it but were
quickly overtaken and captured. Each side suffered
100 casualties. For Perry, who accepted the British
surrender on the deck of the *Lawrence,* it was a bitter-
sweet victory.

Perry put his ships in at West Sister Island, and
while they were under repair, he wrote a report, in
pencil on the back of an envelope, to General William
Harrison, commander of the Army of the Northwest:

> *Dear General: We have met the enemy and they are
> ours. Two ships, two brigs, one schooner and one
> sloop. Yours with great respect and esteem, O. H. Perry*

Perry next sent the following message to the Secretary of the Navy, William Jones:

> *Sir: It has pleased the Almighty to give to the arms of
> the United States a signal victory over their enemies on
> this lake. The British squadron, consisting of two
> ships, two brigs, one schooner, and one sloop, have this
> moment surrendered to the force under my command
> after a sharp conflict. I have the honour to be, Sir, very
> respectfully, your obedient servant, O. H. Perry*

Perry's squadron was quickly returned to action
and ordered to transport 2500 American soldiers to

Detroit to reoccupy the town, which the British under Army Commander Henry Procter had just abandoned. Harrison, with another 1000 troops, intercepted the retreating British and engaged them, killed the Indian leader Tecumseh and won the Battle of the Thames.

For the rest of the war, the Americans controlled Lake Erie. Their naval superiority led to successes on the Niagara Peninsula in 1814 and removed the threat of a British attack on Michigan, Ohio, Pennsylvania or western New York State. But American control was not unthreatened. When they tried to recapture Mackinac Island on Lake Huron they were repulsed. They lost four small ships when the British captured Black Rock at the end of 1813. And four other ships were boarded and captured in separate incidents on Lake Erie and Lake Huron.

Both commanders—Perry and Barclay—faced questions about their handling of the Battle of Lake Erie. Too badly injured to return to active duty, Barclay was absolved of all responsibility for the loss by a court-martial. Meanwhile Perry and Elliot feuded for years, often in the press, about which one failed to execute his responsibilities and therefore was to blame (despite the victory) for the massive damage to the American squadron. As a denouement, the U.S. Navy concluded that both the *Lawrence* and the *Niagara* were too badly damaged to be repaired. They ordered both ships sunk in Misery Bay at Presque Isle on Lake Erie.

～✖～

Rebellions

CHAPTER FIVE

Montgomery's Tavern
December 1837

FOR MANY CANADIANS, THE TALE OF THE American Revolution is simple: the American colonists rose up against the British and engaged in a rebellion that ultimately saw the Americans victorious and free of British control. But few are aware that in 1837, a group of Canadians rebelled against British rule in an attempt to set up a country independent from Britain.

William Lyon Mackenzie emigrated from Scotland to Upper Canada (present-day Ontario) in 1820. Over time he became the publisher of the *Colonial Advocate* newspaper. He quickly established a reputation as being an extreme radical, ready to goad the political and financial elites in his pursuit of political reform. Through his paper, he won enough popular support to be elected to the Legislative Assembly of Upper Canada in 1828, and in 1834 he served one year as Toronto's first mayor.

Despite his electoral success, Mackenzie was faced with the reality that he was making no substantive political change. In July 1836 he lost his legislative seat and returned to the publishing industry with the establishment of another newspaper—the *Constitution*. During the summer of 1837, Mackenzie was elected secretary of the Committee of Vigilance of Upper Canada, which advocated for a Declaration of Independence for Canada modelled on the one used by the Americans.

Focusing his argument on wholesale constitutional change, Mackenzie came to the conclusion that if change was going to happen, it would come only through revolution. In the fall of 1837 elements in Lower Canada (Québec) staged an open revolt against the authorities. Lieutenant-Governor Sir Francis Bond Head decided to send the British regular troops stationed at York (Toronto) to assist in suppressing the revolt in Québec.

Mackenzie recognized that with the British soldiers away, his idea of revolution might succeed in Upper Canada. He convinced John Rolph and Thomas David Morrison, both well-known reformers, that if they struck on December 7, the revolution could succeed without a shot being fired. The government, with no military support to defend it, could not survive. All that was needed was a show of force.

Mackenzie's first action was to seize arms and ammunition from an armoury. He then met with his followers in Stouffville to rally support. The plan was to march the newly armed rebel force down Yonge Street and rendezvous at Montgomery's Tavern just north of Eglington Avenue on December 4. However, when Mackenzie returned to York, he found that Rolph, misled by a false rumour that the British troops were returning to York, had ordered the rebels to move to Montgomery's Tavern ahead of schedule. Mackenzie was livid and demanded that the rebellion stay on his schedule.

Mackenzie realized that he needed information on what the government was planning to do, so he sent some of the rebels forward to do a reconnaissance in force. One group established a roadblock to stop any loyalists from reaching Governor Bond Head and raising an alarm.

Colonel Robert Moodie, a retired militia officer loyal to the government in York, recognized what Mackenzie was planning to do. The colonel pulled together a group of loyalists and made an attempt to break through the rebels' roadblock. When the rebels prevented his advance, Moodie drew his pistol and fired. Numerous rebels returned fire, and Moodie was killed instantly.

Mackenzie had honestly believed that the rebellion would succeed without a shot being fired. The killing of Moodie seemed to drive Mackenzie over the edge, and his plan started to fall apart. Rolph took the opportunity to convince Mackenzie to move up the date of the march to Montgomery's Tavern before the government could mount a response to Moodie's death.

On December 5, Mackenzie led 500 rebels to York City Hall, knowing that a large supply of guns and ammunition was stored there. A truce party met the rebels and tried to convince them to return to their homes. Mackenzie laid out the group's demands, reassuring everyone that if they were met, the rebels would go quietly. Their demands were rejected.

Mackenzie knew he was past the point of no return. He ordered the 1000-strong force to head south on Yonge Street. Twenty-seven loyalists bravely faced the mob, which was armed with rifles, staves and pitchforks. The loyalists fired a volley that was returned by the mob. As the loyalists retreated in the face of the greater numbers, the front line of rebels fired a second volley and then dropped to the ground for cover. To those in the rear, it appeared that their comrades had been killed by loyalist fire. Fearing further shooting, most of the rebels melted into the night and returned to the safety of their homes.

The battle was essentially over. Mackenzie was unable to continue the fight and returned to Montgomery's Tavern. "This was almost too much for human patience," he later wrote. "The city would have been ours in an hour, probably without firing a shot. But 800 ran, and unfortunately the wrong way." The loyalists lost one man in the skirmish and the rebels two, but no one knew what the morning might bring.

Despite the rebels' desperate situation, they vowed to fight on. Anthony van Egmond took command for a despondent Mackenzie and posted 150 men in the woods behind the tavern, 60 more behind a rail fence and the remaining 300 men in front of the tavern. Van Egmond held out little hope that his poorly armed men could turn back government troops and militia. Meanwhile, calls for loyalist reinforcements were sent out, and men soon headed for York from as far away as Hamilton. By the next morning the loyalist forces numbered 1500 and included John A. Macdonald, the future Canadian prime minister.

On December 7, Colonel James Fitzgibbon (of Beaver Dams fame) moved on Montgomery's Tavern with 1000 men supported by artillery. Within minutes of their arrival, the artillery fired on the tavern and terrified the remaining rebels. Fitzgibbon then brought his infantry into the battle and routed the rebels in less than 20 minutes. Following the tradition of victory, Fitzgibbon allowed his men to loot the tavern and then ordered it burned to the ground.

Mackenzie (protected by rebels still supporting the cause), and a number of Americans working for the liberation of Canada, escaped to the United States. Still believing that armed revolution would work, Mackenzie recruited Rensselaer Van Rensselaer III as his new commander. It was a strange choice as Van Rensselaer was a failed West Point student and the nephew of Stephen Van Rensselaer, the U.S. general who was defeated at the Battle of Queenston Heights.

On December 14, in an effort to establish a base of operations away from the prying eyes of American authorities, Mackenzie and Van Rensselaer, supported by 24 rebels, captured Navy Island, a tiny unoccupied island just above Niagara Falls in the Niagara River. There, Mackenzie declared himself

"Chairman Pro. Tem." and the island the "Republic of Canada."

In an attempt to rally recruits to his cause and his odd tricolour flag (adorned with two five-point stars representing Upper and Lower Canada, set above the word "LIBERTY"), Mackenzie offered $100 in silver and 300 acres of "the most valuable lands in Canada" to anyone who would take up arms in his cause. Most of his recruits were Americans who had lost their jobs.

The government of Upper Canada launched a series of formal complaints to the U.S. regarding the build-up of men on Mackenzie's island. Mackenzie further aggravated the Canadians when he ordered his men to start shelling nearby Chippawa. However, the Americans held back, worried that any move on their part would re-ignite a war with Britain. British Colonel Allan MacNab finally grew tired of the military activity emanating from Navy Island, and on December 30 he ordered Captain Andrew Drew to sneak into New York State with a force of men, destroy Mackenzie's supply ship (the SS *Caroline*) and send her remains over Niagara Falls.

In the face of attacks from the British, Mackenzie was forced to withdraw from Navy Island and on January 13, 1838, he fled to the U.S. yet again. This time it was not supporters who greeted him but rather American authorities who promptly arrested him. He was charged with: "...setting on foot a military enterprise at Buffalo, to be carried on against Upper Canada, a part of the Queen's dominions, at a time when the United States were at peace with Her Majesty; with having provided the means for the prosecution of the expedition; and with having done all this within the dominion and territory of the United States." He was found guilty, spent the next 18 months in prison and paid a $10.00 fine.

After his release in May 1840, Mackenzie passed the next 12 years in the United States operating a newspaper and writing. He eventually received an amnesty from Upper Canada and returned to his adopted home in 1850. In 1851 Mackenzie was elected to Parliament and died of an apoplectic seizure 10 years later.

CHAPTER SIX

Fenian Raids
June 1866

IN 1866 AND AGAIN IN 1870, THE movement for a free Ireland took a strange tack by attacking Canada—newly independent from, but still under the protection of, Great Britain. The American Irish Republican Army came up with a plan to use soldiers recently released from the American Federal Army to stage raids into Canada. The theory went that if Canada came under attack, Britain would shift troops there, which would allow for a rebellion in Ireland. At least that was the plan.

In May 1866, the Fenians crossed into Canada. The country's response was slow, as the politicians believed the Fenians posed no real threat. By June 1, the Fenians were highly active in the Fort Erie area, and after they scored a few successes, the entire Canadian militia was called out.

To support the local militia, British General Charles Napier, who was commanding the Canadian Forces, ordered cavalry—the eyes and ears of any army in the 1860s—to the front. Canadian Major George T. Dennison and the Governor General's Body Guard immediately prepared to embark for Fort Erie. On the morning of June 2, the men and horses of the Body Guard moved onto the steamer *City of Toronto*, which transported them across Lake Ontario to the Niagara frontier.

Once their horses and equipment were unloaded, the Body Guard was ordered to proceed to Port Robinson via the Welland Railway. The hard-charging Major Denison took it upon himself to assemble a train and head toward the advancing Fenians. On arrival at Port Robinson, he ordered his men to ride for Chippawa. Here they fed, watered and reshod their horses before continuing forward to New Germany to liaise with Colonel George Peacocke, the area commander.

Peacocke was preparing to lead his column from New Germany when Denison and the Body Guard arrived. Despite having just completed a hard ride, the cavalrymen were ordered to the front of the column with scouts sent out on the right and left flanks. Denison chafed that he could not move faster, but Peacocke ordered him to ride only as fast as the infantry could march. For a cavalry officer, that was a hard order to follow.

The column covered 14 kilometres and halted at Bowen's Farm, some five kilometres northwest of Fort Erie. Peacocke now faced a dilemma: continue to move forward or stop for the night. The bush on the road ahead closed in and provided the perfect place for a Fenian ambush. Denison's forward scouts reported contact with unknown men in the bush less than 180 metres in front of the main column and sent word back that they needed to know what they should do.

Denison led a small force forward to help search for the men. He was convinced that the main Fenian force was on alert. As he noted later, it had grown so dark, "that the men could not, in the woods, see from one to the other; and there being a great deal of tangled bush and logs, and being very marshy and wet, the men could make no headway whatever."

Fearing an ambush, Colonel Peacocke ordered a halt for the night. Despite the darkness, Peacocke once again tried to determine if the enemy was nearby by sending two companies of the 16th Regiment to search the woods. The only thing they found was a bridge that they needed to use, but it was damaged and was impassable. Peacocke recalled the men from the woods and prepared to defend against a night attack. According to the official record:

The 47th Regiment was formed in line to the right of the road, with one company of the same corps about 200 yards in advance, extended as skirmishers. The 10th Royals, of Toronto, were formed up as a support for the 47th, with two companies of that battalion wheeling to the right and extending as skirmishers, so as to fully cover the right flank of the column. The 16th Regiment was placed in a similar position on the left of the road, supported by the Nineteenth Lincoln Battalion, in the same formation. These troops laid in a ploughed field all night, sleeping on their arms, while the guards and sentinels were exceedingly watchful and vigilant. The cavalry and artillery remained in column on the road, with the baggage waggons (sic) in their rear.

Later that evening the St. Catharines Battery of Garrison Artillery (which left its artillery pieces in St. Catharines) joined Peacocke's force and was quickly placed as a rear guard. The Battery, led by Lieutenant James Wilson, had been detailed to protect Chippawa until relieved. Armed with their short Enfield rifles, the soldiers left Chippawa at 4:00 PM and moved quickly to catch up with Peacocke. The officers and men covered 27 kilometres in less than five hours and arrived with every man in his place in the column. They were quickly nicknamed "Stoker's Foot Cavalry," after their commanding officer, and were "formed up across the road, facing to the rear, and after posting the usual guards and sentinels, the remainder were glad to lie down in the dusty road and go to sleep supperless."

All of the men suffered through the cold night. The fact that no fires were allowed because of the proximity of the enemy just added to the misery. The infantry and cavalry had not received any provisions for the campaign, and Major Denison later wrote that:

The want of organization or preparation, in view of the long threatening, seems almost incredible. I had to take my corps on a campaign without the carbines I had asked for, but with revolvers for which we had only some four or five ten-year-old paper cartridges for each. We did not know whether they would go off or not. We had no haversacks, no water bottles, no nose bases (for the horses). Some of us had small tin cups fastened on our saddles. We had no canteens, or knives or forks, or cooking utensils of any kind or valises. We had no clothes except those on our backs. We had no tents and no blankets.

Throughout the night, Colonel Peacocke received information that 2000 or 3000 Fenians had crossed over from the United States as reinforcements, as well as reports on the Canadian losses at the battle of Ridgeway the previous day. Also that night, Lieutenant Colonel John Dennis joined Peacocke and provided details of his defeat at Fort Erie, a fight that also occurred on June 2. For Peacocke, it was one piece of bad news after another, and he told his officers to prepare for a real fight in the morning.

However, at 5:00 AM on June 3, Lieutenant Colonel John Hillyard Cameron rode up to Peacocke's headquarters with the welcome but unbelievable news that the Fenians were in full retreat and leaving Canada for the United States. He also reported that a few small pockets of Fenian stragglers were still putting up some resistance.

Peacocke immediately ordered his men to form up and march on Fort Erie in the hope of catching the retreating Fenians. Major Denison and his cavalry were again ordered to the front to scout for Fenians and send back intelligence. Denison reported that there was evidence throughout the woods and in the village of Fort Erie that the Fenians had been there in full force but were in fact retreating, though "there was still a body of Fenians about the Old Fort, while farmers residing in the neighbourhood said there were a number of stragglers lingering in the woods."

Later the Fenians claimed that British cavalry (actually Denison's forces in the woods) had attacked them the night before. Having no stomach to face what they believed to be a large cavalry force, the poorly trained Americans swiftly decided to retreat across the Niagara River to Buffalo. According to a reporter for the *Buffalo Express* who was with the Fenians: "The retreat was so rapid that rowboats were then crossing the river, evidently propelled with a vigour stimulated by fear. So great was the eagerness to cross that many trusted to a single plank as a means of support, and two small docks on the shore were completely stripped for this purpose."

Denison and his men were beside themselves as they were forced to watch what they believed was a scow full of Fenians escape under the protection of the United States revenue cutter *Michigan*. In fact, the *Michigan* was standing by to arrest the Fenians once they reached shore on the U.S. side.

As the Body Guard advanced down a road littered with Fenian guns, swords and bayonets, Denison himself was involved in catching several Fenian stragglers. Upon sighting a Fenian insurgent trying to escape back to the United States, he and Sergeant John James spurred their horses toward the Niagara

River in hot pursuit. As they crashed around a corner of the trail, the man pushed a rowboat into the river and tried to get the oars in the water. Denison and James swung down from their saddles, drawing and cocking their revolvers as they hit the ground.

"Stand down, come back to shore," ordered Denison. Reluctantly, the man complied. But as James pulled the fugitive out of the boat, the man grabbed for a revolver stuck in the waistband of his pants. "Move and I will blow the top of your head off," said Denison. Something in the steel of Denison's voice told the Fenian that the Canadian Cavalry officer was serious.

James set about searching the boat when a slight movement of canvas caught his eye. The sergeant yanked back the covering and jammed his pistol into a man's terrified face. That was two Fenians taken. But in the excitement, neither Denison nor James noticed a third man approach from the rear. "Stop!" shouted the man, as Denison and James spun, levelling their pistols at this new target. "We're no Fenians," ventured the man, eyeing the pistols warily.

Denison raised his pistol to the man's eye. "If you are not Fenians why do you have pistols and why are there Fenian rifles and bayonets in your boat?" By way of an answer, the men surrendered immediately.

With the three prisoners disarmed, Denison and James mounted their horses while keeping their pistols trained on their quarry. Soon the little parade was headed back to the Canadian headquarters—the three Fenians stumbling up the road ahead of Denison, James and their horses.

For the next three weeks, Denison and the Body Guard did outpost and patrol duties at Fort Erie. On June 20, with the danger passed, the entire Canadian force was ordered home. Many of the men carried captured Fenian rifles and other war trophies through the crowded streets of Toronto, where the populace greeted them with cheers and waving handkerchiefs.

CHAPTER SEVEN

Duck Lake
March 1885

IN 1870, LOUIS RIEL, IN AN ATTEMPT to challenge the authority of the Canadian government in the newly formed province of Manitoba, led the Red River Rebellion. Defeated by a force of Canadian soldiers, Riel was driven into exile in Montana.

By 1884 Riel was back in Canada—this time in the South Saskatchewan River Valley near Batoche. During the spring of 1885, Riel established a provisional government and, seeing himself as a saviour of the Native people, called on both the Natives and Métis to rise up in rebellion against the government of Canada. Leading the fight was the Métis Gabriel Dumont.

Dumont was born in Assiniboia in 1838 and raised on the plains of western Canada. Unable to read and write, he was nonetheless a born leader, an expert buffalo hunter and respected by everyone who ever met him. Dumont played almost no role in the Red River Rebellion of 1870, but by 1884 he felt that the Canadian government was abusing the rights of the Métis. Dumont travelled to Montana to convince Riel to return to Canada and fight. By March 1885, the Métis were starting to answer Riel's call for rebellion.

At the same time, North West Mounted Police Superintendent Leif Crozier was in charge of the old Hudson's Bay Company post at Fort Carlton, 65 kilometres from Prince Albert. When an Indian agent named Lash was kidnapped by a group of Métis, and private storehouses across the territory were raided, Crozier telegraphed NWMP Commissioner A.G. Irvine for assistance.

Fearing that the telegraph lines might be down, Crozier also sent Joseph McKay, an English-Métis interpreter, to Prince Albert to request a relief force of 80 volunteers. The people of Prince Albert, who also feared the rebellion forming around them, quickly stepped forward to help stop the Métis. Soon Captain Moffatt, commander of the Militia at Prince Albert, had sworn in a large crowd of volunteers and, "much excitement and enthusiasm prevailed, though the universal impression was that nothing more than a show of force would prove necessary." As the relief force, known as the Prince Albert Volunteers, left for Fort Carlton, the men remaining in Prince Albert were sworn in as home guards and posted around the community as guards and scouts.

The Prince Albert Volunteers reached Fort Carlton unopposed. Crozier quickly organized a mixed force of the Volunteers and his policemen to secure the supply lines back to Prince Albert. Supported by a seven-pound cannon, the men left the fort on March 25, confident they would be successful. However Dumont, upon hearing of the activities of that small force, ordered men from the Regina area to assist the local Métis.

The next day, while on the Beardy Reserve just five kilometres from Duck Lake, Crozier was surprised to see his scout approaching at full gallop, followed by a large party of rebels. In an effort to create a defensive position, Crozier quickly ordered the lead sleighs to be overturned on both sides of the trail. The remaining six sleighs were then brought up and placed into a U-shaped barricade, while the horses were taken to the rear for safety. The Prince Albert Volunteers also spread out along a snow-covered rail fence, though it provided no cover at all.

Sixty metres ahead of Crozier's men, 30 rebels occupied a wooded area and a log house located to their right and 90 metres back. It was a standoff, but Crozier knew his men were in a vulnerable position. Soon a group of rebels led by Falling Sand, a half-blind Cree chief, came forward to talk to Crozier, who used McKay as an interpreter. Crozier stepped forward and demanded to know who they were and what their intentions were. McKay repeated the questions in English, French and Cree. Falling Sand refused to answer and demanded to know the same things of Crozier.

While McKay was distracted, one of the rebels suddenly tried to grab McKay's rifle from his left hand. As McKay freed his rifle, another in Falling Sand's party tried to grab at the pistol in McKay's belt, just as a third pointed a rifle at the interpreter.

Seeing that the situation was deteriorating quickly, Crozier ordered those sheltering behind the sleighs to, "Fire away boys."

McKay freed his pistol and shot and killed his assailant. He and Crozier then dove for cover and reached the sleighs just as both sides opened fire. Despite their precarious position the police and volunteers effectively engaged the enemy, killing or wounding several of Dumont's men. However, Crozier's men were exposed, surrounded on three sides and trapped by deep snow that prevented them from moving. Soon they were suffering causalities of their own.

Crozier's cannon proved effective for the first few minutes of the engagement, despite drawing fire from Dumont's snipers positioned in the log house. Three of the gunners were wounded before they mistakenly put shot into the cannon prior to the powder and rendered the gun inoperable.

> *"As soon as the shooting started," said Dumont, "we fired as much as we could. I myself fired a dozen shots with my Winchester carbine, and I was reloading it to again, when the English alarmed by the number of dead, began to withdraw. It was time they did, for cannon which until then had kept my infantry men from descending the slope, was silenced…."*

Crozier and his men exchanged fire with the rebels for a half hour until it became clear that if any of his force was to survive, they needed to retreat. So he ordered the horses brought forward and harnessed to the sleighs. The men loaded their wounded, reformed the column and started out through the deep snow. "If we had not retreated when we did," wrote Alexander Stewart, who had also been wounded, "we'd all in less than five minutes have been massacred."

Dumont was determined that they would not get away. He shouted to his men, "Courage, I'm going to make the red coats jump in their carts with some rifle shots. And then I laughed not because I took any pleasure in killing, but to give courage to my men."

Throwing caution to the wind, Dumont stood up and was immediately hit by a bullet that grazed his scalp. Knocked to the ground, he struggled to regain his feet as his horse leapt over his prostrate form. "We were then 60 yards from the enemy. I wanted get up, but the blow had been so violent, I couldn't."

Joseph Delorme, one of Dumont's men, cried out that Dumont had been killed. Dumont tried to steady his men by telling them, "Courage, as long as you haven't lost your head you're not dead." He then instructed another man to take his rifle and cartridges so they would not fall into enemy hands. With Dumont down, the rebels were losing the desire to follow Crozier's force.

Riel, who had not taken an active part in the fight, now argued to spare Crozier's men. He approached one of the Dumont brothers, Édouard, who was now in command of Dumont's forces, said that there had been too much bloodshed and asked them, in the name of God, not to kill any more. The words were hardly out of his mouth when one of the rebels shot John Morton, a farmer and captain of the Volunteers, in the back.

Morton, who earlier had killed two of the rebels, screamed in pain and fell mortally wounded to the ground. As the rebels stood over him, he said, "You can't do anything for I am shot through the heart. Take care of my wife and family and tell them that I died like a man on the battlefield." Guillaume Mackay, one of Dumont's men, then drew his pistol and shot Morton in the head.

The battle was over. Crozier's men left nine dead at Duck Lake and suffered 25 wounded, nine of them seriously. At least one man, Charles Newitt, was taken prisoner and held at Duck Lake. As the men in Crozier's command straggled back to Fort Carlton, the relief force of 83 non-commissioned officers and 25 volunteers, led by NWMP Commissioner Irvine, arrived at the fort. Irvine had marched his men from Regina and covered 480 kilometres in a week despite prairie storms and poor trails. They too had faced a hostile force of rebels, but they avoided confrontation by unexpectedly crossing the South Saskatchewan River at a ford.

Irvine had reached Prince Albert on March 24 with every intention of immediately marching to Fort Carlton's relief, not knowing that Crozier had left the safety of the fort to engage the rebels. However, Irvine's men were exhausted, and some suffered various degrees of snow blindness. After discussions with the local authorities, Irvine decided to wait two days before heading out, thereby allowing time for his men and horses to recover.

As they neared Fort Carlton, word reached them that Crozier had marched on Duck Lake and later that he had been routed. Irvine commented that, "I cannot but consider it a matter of regret that, with the knowledge that both myself and my command were within a few miles and en route to Carlton, Superintendent Crozier should have marched out as he did."

It did not take long for Irvine to recognize that no matter how many men he had, Fort Carlton was indefensible. The fort was not a military base but an old trading post built with the protection of hills on three sides. Irvine noted that, "a few determined men, well armed and skilfully using their rifles, could have bottled up a force of 15 or 20 times their number."

Recognizing that the rebels were probably planning an attack on Fort Carlton, Irvine ordered the position abandoned. The next night, March 27, the men started to pack up gear and supplies. In their haste, some hay was dropped near a stove and a fire started. Before it could be brought under control, the fort was in flames, and a large cache of ammunition and supplies was lost. The following day Irvine and his column reached the relative safety of Prince Albert.

~∞~

CHAPTER EIGHT

Batoche
May 1885 ✓

To Canadians living in eastern Canada, it was clear that two Métis rebels—Louis Riel and Gabriel Dumont—were leading an all-out revolt in the west, supported by the Cree and other Natives. At the time, the Canadian government was trying to establish both a stable federal government and a national railway to bind together the new country of Canada. This rebellion threatened all of those plans.

To stop the uprising, Major General Frederick Middleton was ordered to put together the Northwest Field Force and head west to Fort Battleford and Fort Pitt. Middleton, a British regular soldier, was in command of an inexperienced militia mostly from eastern Canada. They faced an enemy that knew the land and was well versed in irregular warfare.

By the time Middleton arrived in the west, the Métis had scored a number of victories that had swollen both their numbers and their morale. Batoche (88 kilometres northeast of Saskatoon in modern-day Saskatchewan) was established as the seat of Louis Riel's Provisional Government as he rallied support for his cause in the region. Riel, the visionary and politician, was supported by Dumont, the great fighter and tactician. Both men were strong-willed and often clashed on how best to wage the war.

Dumont believed that the strength of the Métis and Native forces was based on their hit-and-run tactics that took advantage of the land they knew well. He managed to convince Riel that the best way to defeat Middleton's troops was to move out, engage them and then withdraw before the Canadian soldiers had time to deploy their artillery or machine guns.

Early on the morning of April 24, 1885, Riel and Dumont left Batoche at the head of a group of 200 Métis. Their target was Fish Creek, where Dumont intended to engage a column of Middleton's troops and hopefully defeat them. But just after arriving at Fish Creek, Riel questioned the decision to leave Batoche relatively unguarded. His argument was strengthened when a scout reported that a detachment of Mounted Police had been seen marching in the direction of Batoche. Dumont believed that he could defeat the soldiers at Fish Creek and return to Batoche in time to defend the Métis capital. However, he gave in to Riel's insistent argument and sent 50 Métis back to Batoche with Riel in command.

When the soldiers attacked Dumont at Fish Creek, the wily Métis general managed to draw the enemy into a battle where he held the upper hand. The soldiers had positioned themselves at the top of a small ridge and, as was the practice of the day, fought standing straight up. This silhouetted them against the sun, and Métis sharpshooters killed many of them. The Battle of Fish Creek then ground to a stalemate, though eventually the Métis were forced to withdraw when their ammunition ran low and they came under pressure from the soldiers. Still, for the Métis it was a victory, because it showed the fighters that the white soldiers could be defeated, and it checked Middleton's advance on Batoche.

Dumont returned to Batoche to find that Riel had done little to defend the town. Riel, who was devoutly Roman Catholic, had spent his time discussing religious ideas with the citizens, including his belief that God himself would step in to defend Batoche and the rebellion. While many of the Métis believed Riel, Gabriel Dumont was a more practical man. Dumont agreed with Riel on one point: Middleton did plan to attack Batoche, and he would have an overwhelming force with him. Dumont's scouts reported that the army had about 850 men and artillery. Even as he had rifle pits dug at strategic points around the town, Dumont sent messengers to try to rally both Métis and Natives to the defence of Batoche.

Middleton, however, had learned not to underestimate Dumont. He developed a relatively simple plan to attack and defeat the Métis. He split his force into three columns. Middleton himself led one column and headed for Batoche. He ordered Lieutenant Colonel William Otter to take his column, leave Swift Current and head for Fort Battleford to engage Chief Poundmaker. Finally, he directed Major General Thomas Strange to leave Calgary and head north for Edmonton, where Strange and his men would head down the North Saskatchewan River to attack Chief Big Bear at Fort Pitt.

Middleton's strategy had an immediate effect. When Dumont's messengers arrived at the camps of Poundmaker and Big Bear, they were told that there were no men to spare, as the two chiefs would soon be fighting their own battles with the white soldiers. Dumont was left with only 250 Métis fighters to face Middleton's column.

After the Battle of Fish Creek, Middleton paused for two weeks to give his men time to recover and prepare for the upcoming fight. He took the opportunity to brief his officers. His plan for attacking Batoche involved two distinct movements. If it worked, the town would be surrounded and the Métis cut off from help and supplies. It would then be just a matter of time until Dumont was forced to surrender.

Middleton also had a "secret weapon." Flat-bottomed steamboats plied the rivers of western Canada, delivering goods, livestock and settlers to isolated hamlets and villages across the prairies throughout the later part of the 19th century. When the North-West Rebellion broke out, a number of steamboats were pressed into service in the fight against the rebels. For the attack on Batoche, Middleton planned to have the steamboat *Northcote* take troops downriver past Batoche and unload them beyond the town, so they could attack from one side of the town while the main body of troops attacked from the other.

Middleton was cautious, and on May 7 moved only as far forward as Dumont's farm at Gabriel's Crossing, where he set up his camp for the night. In preparation for its role as a gunboat, the *Northcote* was provisioned with makeshift armour. Using boards from the Métis leader's home and barn, full feed sacks, and even part of Dumont's pool table, the soldiers built defensive positions all over the decks of the *Northcote*. The steamboat was also given some offensive firepower when a small cannon and a new Gatling machine gun were mounted on her decks. Middleton's plan was ready.

The next day he warily moved forward, camped 13 kilometres from Batoche and made his final preparations. On May 9 Middleton ordered the *Northcote* to continue ahead on the South Saskatchewan River. She was to sail past Batoche, land and disgorge her 50 riflemen just as Middleton's force attacked Dumont directly. That was the plan. In fact, he was too cautious and did not advance quickly enough. Worried about a Métis ambush and held up by difficult terrain, he could not keep up with the *Northcote*.

Even as Middleton's men fell behind schedule, the Métis spotted the *Northcote* and opened fire on the steamboat. The improvised armour on the *Northcote* kept the men aboard safe. However, the Métis, who had yet to come under fire from Middleton's slowly advancing force, raced out of their rifle pits and strung a ferry cable across the river. Unable to stop in time, the improvised gunboat rammed into the cable, which sheared off her masts, smokestack and part of the wheelhouse. Out of control, the *Northcote* drifted downriver, taking the riflemen with her. She was out of the battle, and thus ended Canada's first and only inland naval engagement.

Believing his plan was still intact, Middleton continued his advance, completely unaware that no help would be coming from the *Northcote*. His ground forces initially concentrated on capturing the church at Mission Ridge. It was soon clear that no Métis defenders were around the church, and Middleton ordered his cannons to the ridge. From there, Middleton could shell Batoche, so Dumont ordered the women and children to leave the village.

Recognizing the danger that the cannons represented, Dumont ordered them captured. The first tactic the Métis used was highly accurate rifle fire to try to drive the artillerymen from their guns. When this failed, an actual assault was attempted under the cover of smoke from deliberately set bush fires. But Dumont's warriors were held back by fire from the Gatling gun, while the soldiers withdrew the cannons to a safer position. Counterattacks by the soldiers were as ineffective as the Métis sorties.

By the end of the day, the soldiers fell asleep on the ridge; the Métis in their rifle pits. Neither side had made any real advances. Middleton, recognizing that he had again been fought to a stalemate and remembering the lessons of Fish Creek, wrote in his journal that he feared victory was slipping away.

The next morning, Middleton was content to continue his artillery bombardment of the Métis defensive positions and the town of Batoche itself. He ordered a number of half-hearted feints on Métis positions in an attempt to test his enemy's strengths at various points along the line, but his natural cautiousness prevented him from making a full assault. On the Métis side, they were using up valuable ammunition at an alarming rate—with no real success to show for it.

By May 11, Middleton knew that the battle had to be resolved. In a more concerted effort than the day before, he sent a group of men north to probe the Métis flank. At the same time he ordered a general advance that would test the ability of Dumont to simultaneously fight in two places along the line. As the Métis moved to defend their northern flank, they left the main line undermanned. They simply did not have enough men to adequately defend the town. The Canadian soldiers found themselves at the edge of Batoche, virtually unmolested by enemy fire.

But they did not advance because Middleton had seen enough. Ever cautious, he realized the light was failing and that a night attack was much more difficult than a daylight one. The general was happy to fall asleep that night knowing where Dumont was weak and how those weaknesses could be exploited. Middleton knew that Batoche would fall the next day.

Middleton's plan of attack for May 12 was almost identical to his actions of the day before, since the previous assault had shown such promise. One column moved to the north to draw the defenders in that direction. Lieutenant Colonel van Straubenzie then attacked the main defences of the Métis and drove them back into the town.

The soldiers met little resistance, because the Métis were a spent force. By the time of the main attack, fully 75 percent of the defenders had been wounded by artillery fire or had abandoned their posts in the face of what was clearly an inevitable defeat. Those left were generally old men, firing single-shot shotguns, who were tired after days of battle. Ammunition was so low that the Métis loaded their guns with rocks and nails and fired until their black powder ran out.

In a dashing but poorly coordinated frontal assault, the soldiers overran the Métis positions. As the two armies clashed outside of town, those left in Batoche petitioned Riel for the miracle he had promised. When no troops followed behind the main attack, many of the Métis escaped into the surrounding bush, and Riel had his miracle. He and Dumont fled Batoche and hid from the searching troops.

After four days of battle, Middleton was victorious. Those Métis remaining in Batoche surrendered. Several hid for many weeks, worried about reprisals from the soldiers. Over time Métis men and women slowly turned themselves into the army. It was the end of the North-West Rebellion.

As was the tradition at the time, Middleton allowed his men to take what they could from Batoche. Métis properties were looted for anything that was not nailed down. Today it seems a cruel practice, but at the time the soldiers would have expected no less had they been defeated.

With Riel and Dumont in hiding, the priests tried to exert their influence on the situation. Recognizing that Riel's dream was a lost cause, the Catholic clergy in and around Batoche went so far as to refuse to administer the sacraments to those who followed Riel. For the Church, the charismatic Riel was a threat that could not be left unchallenged. For the people, it was all too much.

While hiding from the Canadian soldiers searching for him, Riel was not able to provide guidance to the people who had trusted and followed him. Without their fathers who had joined Riel, many families were now starving and hiding in caves or abandoned buildings. They feared that the soldiers would imprison them as they had done with the men who had taken up arms against the government of Canada.

Dumont was also searching for Riel. Unable to find the rebel leader, Dumont finally gave up and took Riel's wife and two children to his father's home. Isidore Dumont convinced his son that the only safe action was to flee to Montana, where he would be safe from Canadian justice. Gabriel Dumont headed south with Michael Dumas, another Métis leader.

For the soldiers, all that was left was to mop up little pockets of resistance. Poundmaker surrendered on May 23. Big Bear held out until July 2. He had retreated to Loon Lake where he made a last stand against Strange's column. Out of food and ammunition, Big Bear finally surrendered. Middleton and his troops marched north to Prince Albert, and from there they headed home to their business and farms. The *Northcote* was repaired and took the wounded from Batoche to hospitals in Saskatoon.

Gabriel Dumont found peace in the United States. A year after the defeat at Batoche, he joined Buffalo Bill's Wild West Show and performed in front of thousands of people across the U.S. After the Canadian government offered a general amnesty to anyone who had fought in the rebellion, Dumont made his way back to Canada in 1888. He ultimately returned to Batoche and the life of a farmer in 1893.

When Riel was finally located, he offered no resistance to being captured. Rather than trying to flee, he used his time after the Battle of Batoche to pray for divine intervention. He told Middleton that he would give himself up to fulfil God's will and that he wanted freedom for all his council and his people. He would surrender so that he could continue to defend the Métis' cause.

Riel was sent by steamboat to Regina to stand trial for treason. He was found guilty and hung on November 16, 1885.

Foreign
Expeditions

CHAPTER NINE

The Nile Expedition
1884–1885

IT MUST HAVE BEEN A STRANGE SIGHT indeed: 400 French voyageurs, led by a high-society cavalry officer from Toronto, disembarking from a ship in Alexandria, Egypt, ready to row up the Nile River to save a British General trapped in Khartoum, Sudan. For Canada, the Nile Expedition of 1884–85 was the country's first overseas military expedition.

In 1883, facing a widespread revolt in Sudan, Britain decided to relinquish its control of the country and ordered General Gordon, the former Governor General of Sudan, to oversee the evacuation of soldiers, civilians and their families and then return to England. But as the situation deteriorated, Gordon decided to stay in Khartoum to defend the city with his 6000 men.

By mid-March 1884, the Mahdist rebel army had stopped all river traffic and cut off the city from the outside world. The British government, fearing both the cost and danger of relieving the city, decided not to attempt a rescue of Gordon and his men. But by August, British public opinion for a rescue had grown so strong that the government relented and ordered General Garnet Wolseley to Khartoum.

Wolseley decided to ascend the Nile River by boat. Based on his experiences during the Red River Rebellion in Canada in 1870, he requested a force of Canadian voyageurs be made available to row to Gordon's rescue. He turned to another Canadian, his former aide-de-camp Lieutenant Colonel Frederick C. Denison (brother of Lieutenant Colonel George T. Denison; see "Fenian Raids"), to recruit and lead the force. Since the voyageurs were volunteers paid for by the British, the Canadian government agreed to the overseas mission.

By September 15, 1884, 386 voyageurs—86 of them from various Native Canadian tribes—had signed up for six months of service and were on their way to Egypt. Denison and his force of Canadians met Wolseley at Wadi Halfa, Egypt, on October 26 and saw for the first time the modified Royal Navy whalers they were to use to row up the Nile and through the remaining five of the Nile's six major cataracts.

The Canadians soon discovered just how difficult the task was. Progress was slow because they were often under rebel attack and at times were forced to manhandle the large boats through rapids and against the current. In November, upon hearing that Khartoum might soon fall, Wolseley split his force in two—half headed overland while the remainder, including the Canadians, continued up the Nile.

After six months of struggle, the voyageurs still had not reached Khartoum. In March 1885, with their original commitment completed, only Denison and 85 of the voyageurs re-enlisted; the others decided to return to Canada. In the meantime, on January 26, 1885, the Mahdist army breached the defences of Khartoum. Gordon and his army were slaughtered. Two days later Wolseley's overland relief force reached the city, but they were too late.

The British forces fell back to Egypt; the Nile Expedition had failed. On April 17, 1885, the last of the Canadians headed for home. Canada's first foreign military expedition cost 16 lives and earned her the thanks of Great Britain.

CHAPTER TEN

Paardeberg, South Africa
February 1900

LIEUTENANT COLONEL FREDERICK DENISON and his 386 voyageurs were the first Canadians to take part in a foreign military expedition. However, the first Canadians to participate in an actual battle overseas were the men and officers of the 2nd Battalion, Royal Canadian Regiment of Infantry (2 RCRI), who fought at Paardeberg in distant South Africa.

The Boer War was about differing visions and life-styles. The British saw South Africa as a vast, rich region that would provide wealth and glory. To the Boers, South Africa was home, and the British were intruders. The scene was set for conflict. When Great Britain declared war on the Boers, Canada followed suit. On October 30, 1899, 41 officers and 962 men of the 2 RCRI, under the command of Lieutenant Colonel William Otter, embarked for South Africa.

Upon arrival, Otter completed the training of his Canadians while the Boers laid siege to Ladysmith, Kimberley and Mafeking. The British knew that if they were to be successful in South Africa, they first had to lift the sieges and free the citizens of the three communities. On February 8, 1900, the Canadians were ordered to join the 19th Brigade along with the

1st Gordon Highlanders, 2nd Shropshire Light Infantry and the Duke of Cornwall's Light Infantry. All were under the command of Major General Horace Smith-Dorrien.

The plan was to relieve Kimberly by first marching 67 kilometres to the Modder River. Then the British forces would outflank the Boers, capture the fords and break the siege. On February 13, a vast column of men, horses, wagons and cattle set out across the veldt. The land was open grassland dotted with kopjes (small rocky hills), rocks and rivers. Dust choked the men as they walked, and their water supplies quickly ran out. The Canadians foraged for water but found only brackish, muddy rivers with incredibly steep banks. Otter was starting to realize how difficult the campaign would be when word reached him that the Boers, in a daring raid, had captured one-third of the column's supply wagons. Not only was water in short supply, but biscuits and bully beef were as well.

Three days after their departure, the men of the 2 RCRI celebrated the news that Kimberly had been relieved. But at the same time, 5000 Boers withdrew to a safer location at Paardeberg Hill, where they built a defensive position consisting of trenches cut into the ground and wagons linked together. Three hundred metres above them towered Paardeberg Hill. To their south, on the Modder River, was the ford known as Paardeberg Drift. Stretching back from the river were rows of rocks that provided both cover and obstacles for the attacking British and Canadian troops.

As they chased the Boers, the 2 RCRI reached Klip's Drift on the Riet River on February 17. After a brief rest, the Canadians pushed on through the night and reached Paardeberg Drift the next morning.

Along with the Shropshires and Gordons, the 2 RCRI were to cross the Modder at Paardeberg Drift. Otter ordered A and C Companies forward, with D and E Companies in support. Four other companies, including B Company, formed his reserves. The crossing should have been easy since the water level in the Modder was supposed to be low, but the Boers had broken a dam upstream, which forced the men to struggle across through shoulder-high water levels.

By 10:00 AM, the eight companies of the 2 RCRI were clear of the river and heading east toward the Boer trenches. Along with the British units, the Canadians were to take part in a direct frontal assault on the Boer positions. But the terrain was challenging as it did not allow for easy communications, and at times Otter and the Canadians did not even know where their senior officers were.

Suddenly, and seemingly out of nowhere, the Canadians came under fire from the Boer Mausers (bolt-action rifles). Unable to locate the source of the attack, some of the Canadians continued to run toward the sound of the guns, while others crawled in search of cover among the rocks and anthills. Casualties started to mount.

By noon the men were pinned down by sniper fire and running out of water. Just when it seemed things could not get any worse, the sky opened up and the men were doused by a passing storm. When the rains lifted at 3:00 PM, Otter headed out in search of further orders. Unable to locate Major General Smith-Dorrien, he returned to find his officers and the chaplains filling in for wounded stretcher-bearers. While Otter and his men tried to hold their position, the British cavalry from Kimberley was sent to relieve the pressure on the Canadians by surrounding the Boers.

With the Canadians pinned down and the cavalry still not in position, Smith-Dorrien—frustrated by the apparent lack of movement—ordered the Cornwalls to the north side of the Modder to support the Canadians and to attack. At 4:00 PM, three and a half companies of the Cornwalls were in position. Smith-Dorrien found Otter and spared no language in describing how little he thought of the worthless Canadian troops, whom he felt were not attacking with enough vigour. He then ordered a bayonet charge and the Cornwalls rose up. Not to be outdone, the 2 RCRI also fixed their bayonets and charged the enemy position. Smith-Dorrien later reported that there was confusion everywhere on the battlefield:

At 5:15 p.m. I was horrified at seeing our troops on the right of my line rise and charge forward with a ringing cheer. I, at that time, believed that only Canadians were there; but…Lieut.-Col. Aldworth, D.S.O.… had been sent over by a higher authority to charge the Boer position, and that the Canadians, who would not be left behind, had joined in.

Ahead of the Canadians lay 450 metres of open ground. They did not make it all the way. They managed 180 metres before they were forced to take cover. With the Boers closing in on the left flank, Otter knew he had little choice but to withdraw. Some men volunteered to stay and collect the wounded and dead. Harassed by Boer sniper fire, the last stretcher party returned to camp at 2:00 AM the next morning. The Canadians suffered 18 killed and 64 wounded.

For the British it was much worse. As dawn broke on the morning of February 19, British casualties were 1300, while the Boers had lost only 300. However, British artillery had killed most of the Boers' horses and cattle.

The Boers asked for a temporary truce so they could bury their dead, but not wanting to give the enemy time to regroup, the British High Command refused the request and prepared to again engage the Boers. This time, however, there would be no frontal attack but rather a siege designed to starve the enemy into submission. The plan was simple. British heavy artillery would continue to pound the Boers. Meanwhile, British infantry dug trenches toward the

Boers' positions, which would allow the men to stay behind cover as they attacked.

The next day found the 2 RCRI frantically digging trenches north of the Modder in an attempt to reach the Boer position. The Canadians suffered from both thirst and hunger. At one point Otter tried to get a water cart to his thirsty men, but the Boers immediately opened fire on the cart with a machine gun. Throughout February 21 and 22 the Canadians worked on trenching. The only way the men could tell the difference between the days was that on the second day a chilling rain fell. For the 2 RCRI this was especially trying as they had only one blanket per two men. Even in the trenches the casualties mounted, thanks to the Boer snipers.

But by February 26 the Boers were in desperate straits. They were short of food and water, their casualties were mounting and the risk of disease from the rotting animal carcasses was rising. Even to the Boers, it was clear that no help was coming, and the British trenches were getting ever closer. On the British side, orders were prepared—there was to be an attack on the Boers at dawn the next day.

At 1:45 AM the Canadians woke and headed out of the trenches. It was so dark they were forced to hold hands so as not to become separated. The plan called for them to be in position for the assault within 25 minutes of their departure, but that was a very optimistic estimate. When there was no evidence of an attack, British and Canadian reinforcements were sent to find the "lost" Canadians.

In fact, the Canadians were not lost, and at 2:50 AM they made contact with the Boers. The Canadians came under heavy fire from only 60 metres away. As the first rank returned fire, the second rank of 2 RCRI dug an advance trench on the high ground some 85 metres from the Boer position, which gave the Canadians the advantage of height. On the south side of the Modder River, a second Canadian contingent was also digging an advance trench.

As dawn broke, the Boers moved dangerously close to the Canadians on the river's south side. But confusion was growing due to communication breakdowns on both sides of the river. On the north side the Canadians thought they heard an order to retire, and rather than holding the line, they started to evacuate their wounded. Others members of the 2 RCRI settled into the new trench on the river's south side and opened fire on the Boers.

At sunrise a call went out to the Boers to surrender, as they were now under direct fire from the Canadian positions. Within minutes, one white handkerchief appeared. Then more and more were held up by the Boers. A cheer rose from the Canadian side when a large white sheet was hoisted over the main Boer position. The fighting was over. The official surrender was signed on February 28.

The February 27 battle cost Otter six killed and 21 wounded; the Boers lost 70 with 200 wounded. Total

Canadian losses from the time of their February 18 arrival at Paardeberg Drift were 12 dead and 37 wounded. Most damaging to the Boer cause were the 5000 rifles, the large stock of ammunition and the 4200 prisoners—some 10 percent of their army—captured by the British.

The 2 RCRI were happy to leave Paardeberg and return to their clean, new camp at Eerste Fabriken, a garrison east of Pretoria. They were happier still to return to Canada, in October 1900, at the end of their year of service in South Africa.

World War I

CHAPTER ELEVEN

Vimy Ridge
April 1917

IF ANY BATTLE IS FAMILIAR TO CANADIANS, it is Vimy Ridge. Vimy was the first time the Canadian Corps fought together, the first time they captured a position that no other army was able to take, and the first time Canada's Army fought as professionals.

To the rest of the world, the Battle of Vimy Ridge was a relatively small action in the much larger Battle of Arras, which itself was a diversionary attack for the French Nivelle Offensive. The Canadians faced the German Sixth Army in the Nord-Pas-de-Calais region of France. The objective was to capture Vimy Ridge, a seven-kilometre-long escarpment that rises to a height of 145 metres. Located eight kilometres northeast of Arras, Vimy Ridge had been held by the German Army since they first took it in 1914. The Canadians were expected to gain and hold the ridge to prevent the Germans from firing on the Allied troops advancing in the Arras offensive.

Vimy Ridge proved to be a tough problem for the Allies. During the Second Battle of Artois in May 1915, the French 1st Moroccan Division actually reached the top of the ridge, but the Germans pushed them off when French reinforcements failed to

appear. The French tried to capture the ridge four
months later during the Third Battle of Artois. While
they did take the town of Souchez at the western
base of the ridge—at a cost of 150,000 casualties—it
was as far as the French went.

In February 1916, Lieutenant General Sir Julian
Byng and the British XVII Corps relieved the French
Army, giving them a much-needed rest. For the British, battle was quick to come. On May 21, they faced
a concerted German attack that saw a number of
positions lost along the 1800-metre front. Until the
newly formed Canadian Corps relieved the British in
October 1916, there was no further advance against
the ridge itself.

The Canadian Corps was under the command of
British Lieutenant General Sir Julian Byng. While
Byng knew as early as May 1916 that the Corps'
objective was Vimy Ridge, a formal plan was not
accepted until nearly a year later. For the Canadians,
this was to be the first time all four divisions fought
together. Supported by the British 5th Infantry Division, and reinforced by artillery, engineer and labour
units, the attacking force had 170,000 officers and
men—97,184 of them Canadians. Arrayed against
Byng's four attacking divisions and one division of
reserves was the Sixth Army of General Ludwig von
Falkenhausen with 20 line divisions (plus reserves)
responsible for the Cambrai to Lille sector.

As Byng and his officers studied the ridge, the plan
they devised was relatively simple. The Canadians

would attack along a front 6400 metres long. The first tasks were to seize the German forward line, then capture of the town of Thelus and the German second line. The final actions would end with the heavily fortified knoll known as "the Pimple," the Folie Farm, the Zwischen-Stellung trench and the hamlet of Les Tilleuls in Canadian hands.

The plan called for 24 brigade artillery groups to provide one heavy gun every 18 metres and one field gun every nine metres, firing a total of 1.6 million shells. The light artillery was to provide a creeping barrage that advanced in 90-metre increments to protect the infantry. The heavy artillery was to concentrate on clearing German defensive positions before the infantry even reached them. The infantry would have to move quickly to keep up with the barrages and would "leapfrog" each other during the advance.

Byng and his senior staff were convinced that the Canadians could take Vimy Ridge. However, they were not willing to leave anything to chance. Byng insisted that the men of the Canadian Corps practice each and every step to be taken on the battlefield. Well behind the front lines, training officers laid out full-scale models of sections of the battlefield, with taped lines representing enemy trenches. Officers on horseback marked where the artillery barrage would be and when it would occur. Each man was expected to have the timing down exactly.

For the first time, soldiers were trained not just for their own jobs but also for those of the men above and below them. Platoon sergeants and section commanders were given maps to ensure they knew the exact layout of the battlefield, which gave them a much better understanding of their upcoming tasks. Byng was determined that poor command and control would not be the reason for failure at Vimy. For the officers, the training was no less vigorous. A large-scale model of the battlefield was built at British First Army Headquarters that allowed the officers to study each German trench and defensive position in minute detail.

As the infantry training continued above ground, British and Canadian tunnelling companies and engineers were digging extensive tunnels under the battlefield itself. The soft chalk of France was hollowed out at a depth of 10 metres, creating 12 "subways" up to 1.2 kilometres in length. The tunnel system was so extensive that light-rail lines, hospitals, command posts, water reservoirs, ammunition stores, mortar and machine gun posts, and communication centres were built into them. The tunnels stretched from the reserve lines to the front lines, thereby allowing troops to move forward in relative safety.

Byng brought other new methods to the battlefield at Vimy. He had the engineers dig 13 tunnels under the German positions and ordered them packed with thousands of kilograms of high explosives in an effort to destroy the defences on the Pimple and near the Broadmarch crater. Trench raiding became a Canadian specialty. Byng recognized that the raids, first employed to capture prisoners and gather intelligence, could also be used to train the Canadian soldiers to attack static defences. Altogether the Canadians launched 55 raids before the day of the attack.

Finally, the Royal Flying Corps (RFC) established a two-to-one superiority in the air. The RFC provided both visual spotting of the enemy and aerial photography, which allowed planners on the ground to better understand the German defences and the locations of equipment and men in the opposing trenches. It proved pivotal to the success at Vimy.

On March 20, Byng ordered the artillery to begin a two-week preliminary bombardment of trenches, German batteries and strong points. The actual battle for Vimy Ridge began at exactly 5:30 AM on April 9, 1918. Under a cold and snowy sky, every artillery piece opened fire simultaneously, followed 30 seconds later by massive explosions as the mines under the German positions were detonated. Thousands of German soldiers were killed instantly and their defences laid to waste.

Next the creeping barrage began, advancing 90 metres every three minutes. By 6:25 AM, the 1st, 2nd and 3rd Canadian Divisions had already captured their initial objectives. The 4th Division was held up by fierce German resistance and took some hours to reach its targets.

For the Canadians in the 1st, 2nd and 3rd Divisions, the advance continued. By 7:00 AM, the 1st Division was in possession of the left half of the Red

Line and supported the 1st Canadian Brigade as it moved through and captured the rest of the Red Line. At the same time, the 2nd Division seized the town of Les Tilleuls. At 7:30 AM, the 3rd Division was at the western edge of the Bois de la Folie.

However, the rapid advance of the 3rd Division caused it some difficulty, as the 4th had still not captured Hill 145, which left the 3rd flank exposed. At 9:00 AM, the 7th Canadian Brigade of the 3rd Division was rushed up to protect the exposed flank. The Canadians settled down in the shell holes and ruined trenches to consolidate their positions and prepare for the next day.

On the morning of April 10, reinforcements from the 1st and 2nd Divisions moved up. Their job was to leapfrog those units now on the Red Line and move through to the Blue Line. The 2nd Division received help from two sections of tanks and the 13th British Brigade. By 11:00 AM, the 2nd Division had taken Hill 135 and Thelus.

For 90 minutes the advance halted and the barrage remained stationary as machine guns were brought forward to support the infantry. By 1:00 PM the 1st and 2nd Divisions were moving forward again—this time toward the Brown Line, the final objective. At 2:00 PM, both divisions were securing their positions on the Brown Line. By 3:15 PM, the 10th Canadian Brigade had secured Hill 145. For the Canadians, the only position unconquered on Vimy Ridge was the Pimple.

During the night the Canadians prepared for the assault on the Pimple. The Royal Engineers brought forward Livens Projectors, mortars used to deliver poison gas, and pumped 40 drums of mustard gas into the nearby town of Givenchy-en-Gohelle, while artillery harassed the enemy through the night. At 5:00 AM on April 12, the 10th Canadian Brigade, supported by the 24th British Division, pushed forward into a west wind and driving snow. Thirteen hours later the Pimple, defended by German troops in hastily built trenches and dugouts, was in Canadian hands. The Battle of Vimy Ridge was over.

The Canadian Corps suffered 10,602 casualties—3598 killed and 7004 wounded. Four members of the Corps earned the Victoria Cross. On the German side, an unknown number were killed or wounded, and 4000 were taken prisoner.

For the Canadians and the Allies, the taking of Vimy Ridge was of huge importance. The Canadians proved they could fight as a group and do the difficult tasks. For the Germans, Vimy Ridge forced them to reassess their defensive strategy in the area. Rather than counterattacking, the German High Command ordered a scorched-earth policy where every building and crop was destroyed by the retreating German forces as they moved back to the Oppy-Méricourt line. For the rest of the war the Allies held Vimy Ridge.

CHAPTER TWELVE

Passchendaele
October 1917

... I died in Hell (they called it Passchendaele) my wound was slight and I was hobbling back; and then a shell burst slick upon the duckboards; so I fell into the bottomless mud, and lost the light.

–Siegfried Sassoon

BY THE SPRING OF 1917, IT WAS CLEAR THAT the Allies were in trouble. They faced convoy attacks by German submarines, and the collapse of Czarist Russia potentially freed one million additional German troops to fight on the Western Front. Mutinies by French soldiers threatened the very existence of a French army. The Allies desperately needed a victory.

Trying to keep pressure on General Erich Ludendorff and the Imperial German Army, British General Sir Douglas Haig planned for a sweeping breakthrough in Flanders that would see the Germans driven back, the submarine bases in Belgium captured and the French armies given a chance to recover their morale. Haig's plan pivoted around the Belgian town of Ypres. If the Passchendaele Ridge could be taken and the town liberated, the British could turn north and the Belgian coast would be open to them.

The First Battle of Ypres in 1914 and the Second Battle of Ypres a year later saw the Germans attacking the Allies. In 1917, the Allies attacked a strongly entrenched enemy that was ready and waiting for them.

In late May 1917, Allied artillery bombarded the German defences on the Messines Ridge southeast of Ypres. At 2:50 AM on June 7, the shelling abruptly ceased, and 10,000 German troops were killed when 450,000 kilograms of explosives, packed into tunnels under the ridge, were detonated. The British infantry raced up the ridge to find almost no opposition left. However, British General Charles Plumer failed to press home the advantage, and the delay allowed the German Army to rebuild its defences.

Despite the lost opportunity, Haig was convinced a breakthrough was possible. On July 18 the British artillery opened fire, with approximately 3000 guns dropping more than four million shells on the German positions during the next 12 days. At 3:50 AM on July 31, British troops charged forward to start the Battle of Pilckem Ridge.

The shelling destroyed creeks and drainage canals just as the worst rains in 30 years started to fall. Men struggled through the clinging mud. Weighed down with more than 24 kilograms of equipment, men who slipped off the wooden duckboards (walkways) often drowned. Their comrades were ordered not to even attempt a rescue as the drowning man often pulled his rescuers in with him. In taking 1800 metres, the Allies suffered 32,000 casualties.

On August 16 conditions finally improved enough for the British to continue the attack. The four days of fighting during the Battle of Langemarck saw few gains. The Germans suffered as well. According to Ludendorff:

> *The costly August battles imposed a heavy strain on the Western troops. In spite of all the concrete protection they seemed more or less powerless under the enormous weight of the enemy's artillery. At some points they no longer displayed that firmness which I, in common with the local commanders, had hoped for.*

The British now had 1295 guns, one for every five metres of the attack front, firing on the German positions. On September 20, the British suffered 21,000 casualties at the Battle of Menin Road. Wave after wave of German counterattacks crashed on the British positions, but the troops held the 1400 metres they had captured. In the Battle of Polygon Wood (September 26 to October 3), British troops gained 2000 metres at the cost of 30,000 casualties. It was now imperative that Passchendaele Ridge be captured quickly, because the British found themselves directly under it—and German artillery fire.

On October 4 the Australians managed to capture Passchendaele Ridge at the Battle of Broodseinde— the high point for the Allies in early October. Five days later the Allied forces were ordered to take the town of Poelkapelle. The battle was a total failure.

Any advances made were soon lost to German counter-attacks. By October 12 the Allies had suffered 13,000 casualties, and the attacks were called off.

In the face of 100,000 casualties, Haig decided that the British, Australian and New Zealand troops, on whom he had relied so far, could do no more. He turned to the Canadians. Lieutenant General Sir Arthur Currie, a former Victoria businessman and militia officer who was now Commander of the Canadian Corps, objected strongly. The British High Command insisted that Passchendaele was worth the effort, and Haig personally convinced Currie to accept the challenge.

Knowing that advance preparation, particularly at Vimy, had led to the Canadian Corps successes, Currie insisted that there would be no attack on Passchendaele until he personally felt the men were ready. He also demanded that the Canadians be allowed to leave the salient once the battle was over. Currie was determined that Canadian lives would not be spent both attacking and defending Passchendaele.

Currie personally inspected the battlefield and predicted that the Canadians would be successful, but at a cost of 16,000 casualties. Major Robert Massie of the Canadian Artillery reported on his first visit to the battlefield.

The first day I went in, the mud was 6 inches deep everywhere, and in most places half way up to my knees. It would dry up sometimes, but would always rain afterwards and be worse than ever. The

*surrounding country was literally shot to pieces, look-
ing like a field after trees and stumps have been pulled
out, except that the holes are as deep as 10 feet and
filled with water. The lips of one shell hole practically
touched the lips of another, so that horses and mules
could not go across the area. The first lot would get
across, but half a dozen following would soon turn the
whole thing into a mass of water and mud so that the
animals could not make it at all.*

Everyone in the forward areas was under constant
enemy observation and bombardment. Even as specialized troops known as pioneer units built new
roads and bridges for the Canadian infantry, German
bomber aircraft (a relatively new phenomenon on
the Western Front) dropped explosives on the men
and their work. Altogether 1500 Canadians were
killed before the battle even began.

Currie laid out a simple and straightforward plan
to take Passchendaele. The Canadians would attack
in a series of coordinated operations, each with
a limited objective, until the village and a defensible
position on the Passchendaele Ridge were gained.

From October 12 to 25, 587 Allied guns shelled
German positions. Rolling barrages moved across
no-man's-land—and stopped, only to start again.
The Germans, crouching in their pillboxes and dugouts, could not tell when the actual assault was to
begin. Unlike in the past, this time surprise was on
the Canadians' side.

At 5:40 AM on October 26, Canadian heavy machine guns opened fire. Two minutes later every gun in the Canadian batteries fired simultaneously. Press reports later noted the opening barrage could be heard in London. Pillboxes and barbed wire were blown out of the way. A total of 20,000 Canadians crawled out of dugouts and trenches, advancing under a mist that quickly turned to rain. The rolling barrage provided some protection, but it moved so quickly and was so complex that it allowed German gunners time to target the advancing Canadians.

The 3rd and 4th Divisions attacked over low ground prior to reaching the higher ground on the other side. The 3rd Division crept ahead crater to crater. Lewis machine-gun teams were called up when the fighting was particularly heavy, but soon the Canadians were on the Red Line east and north of Passchendaele itself.

The 4th Division made it even farther. However, the Germans responded the next day with heavy counterattacks that ultimately drove the Canadians out of the newly captured Decline Wood. During the night of October 27–28 the Canadians retook Decline Wood after intense hand-to-hand combat, often at bayonet point.

During the next two days the Canadians dug in to hold onto their gains. To reach this point, seven battalions lost a total of 2481 men. Private Richard Mercer summed up the fighting:

*Passchendaele was just a terrible, terrible, terrible,
terrible, terrible, terrible place. We used to walk along
these wooden duckboards—something like ladders
laid on the ground. The Germans would concentrate
on these things. If a man was hit and wounded and
fell off he could easily drown in the mud and never be
seen again. You just did not want [to] go off the
duckboards.*

On October 30, the Canadians began the assault
on Passchendaele Ridge. Currie's strategy of taking
and holding small gains was working. Together with
two British Divisions the Canadians, under the cover
of a driving rainstorm, quickly got to the outskirts of
the now-ruined village of Passchendaele. For five
days, often up to their waists in mud and under
intense German artillery fire, the Canadians held
on, waiting for relief. By the time the 1st and 2nd
Divisions relieved the embattled troops, 80 percent
of the 3rd and 4th Divisions were casualties.

On November 6, following hand-to-hand fighting,
the 2nd Division easily occupied Passchendaele after
only three hours of battle. The 1st Division, however,
found itself in some trouble as one company of the
3rd Battalion was cut off and stranded in a bog.
When the situation righted itself, 1st Division
continued toward its objectives. By the end of the
day the Canadian Corps was firmly in control of
Passchendaele and the ridge.

The Canadians' final action at Passchendaele
started at 6:05 AM on November 10. Currie used the

opportunity to make adjustments to the line, strengthening his defensive positions. The Canadians had done the impossible. After only 14 days they had driven the German Army out of Passchendaele and off the ridge. But there was almost nothing left of the town to hold. Altogether the Canadian Corps had fired 1,453,056 shells or 41,564 tonnes of high explosives. Aerial photography showed one million shell holes inside a space of 2.5 square kilometres.

For the Canadians, Currie's words were prophetic. He had told Haig it would cost Canada 16,000 casualties to take Passchendaele—in truth it took 15,654. One thousand Canadian bodies were never recovered, trapped forever in the mud of Flanders. Nine Canadians won the Victoria Cross.

Haig was true to his word. By November 14, 1917, the Canadians were back in the relative quiet of the Vimy region. They were not asked to hold what had cost so much to take. Sadly, in March 1918, all of the gains made by Canada at Passchendaele were lost during the German spring offensive.

CHAPTER THIRTEEN

Billy Bishop's Air War
1917–1918

UNTIL THE START OF WORLD WAR I, THE gallant and dashing officers and men were all in the cavalry—at least that was the common perception. But in the mud of France and Belgium, the cavalry was stalled behind the lines, with men and horses condemned to endless training and grooming. There were few grand charges and even fewer cavalry victories.

For men committed to the ideal of dash and élan, the new military specialty of aviation beckoned. Once again the individual could make a difference with one-on-one combat, this time high above the earth. William Avery "Billy" Bishop came to represent the Knights of the Air.

Born in 1894 in Owen Sound, Ontario, Bishop never really seemed to fit in despite being the son of upper middle-class parents. He stayed away from team sports and focused instead on individual activities such as swimming, horse riding and shooting. His grades throughout his school career were poor—poor enough that he did not qualify for admission to the University of Toronto.

With few other options open to him, Bishop enrolled at Kingston's Royal Military College (RMC) in 1911. Legend has it that he was expelled from the RMC, but in fact he was forced to repeat the first year of a three-year program because he was found guilty of the "use of any improper means of obtaining information relative to an examination." During the autumn of 1914, Bishop was preparing for his final year at Kingston. However, rather than miss the grand adventure unfolding in Europe, he withdrew from the college and enlisted in the army.

For Bishop there was only one branch of the army—the cavalry. He joined and was commissioned an officer in the Mississauga Horse. Much to his disappointment, he was diagnosed with pneumonia in October 1914 and not allowed to go to Europe with the regiment. Instead he was reassigned to the 7th Canadian Mounted Rifles. Bishop's shooting and riding experience (as a young boy) made him a natural in the mounted infantry unit.

The Rifles shipped out on June 6, 1915, aboard the S.S. *Caledonia*. On June 21, off the coast of Ireland, two of the ships in Bishop's convoy were sunk and some 300 Canadians died. However, the *Caledonia* was unscathed and arrived in Plymouth Harbour on June 23.

The realities of trench warfare soon wore on the young Canadian even as he started training in England. He had not signed up to slog through the mud as an infantryman. By July 1915 he was already focusing on a flying career: "...it's clean up there! I'll bet you don't get any mud or horseshit on you up

there. If you died, at least it would be a clean death."
It turned out that the Royal Flying Corps had an
overabundance of pilots but needed observers for
reconnaissance aircraft. It wasn't piloting, but it was
a way out of the trenches. Bishop was soon a member
of the Corps.

On September 1 he was sent to 21 (Training)
Squadron at Netheravon for elementary air instruc-
tion. In early 1916 he flew numerous missions in
France before being involved in a crash that left him
injured and recuperating in a hospital in England.
After spending most of 1916 in England, Bishop used
his family's connections to apply for pilot training,
and in November he earned his wings.

His first assignment was to fly over London searching for German zeppelins to shoot down. He hated
the tedium of defensive flying and was soon lobbying
to be transferred to France.

On March 17, 1917, Bishop found himself assigned
to 60 Squadron at Filescamp Farm near Arras,
France. The odds of survival were not good. He
started flying the obsolete Nieuport 17 just as the
Germans were shooting down five British planes for
every one they lost. The average lifespan for a rookie
pilot in 60 Squadron was 11 days.

Five days later, while flying a mission in the Nieuport, Bishop was nearly shot down by German
anti-aircraft fire. Then he became separated from his
group and had to find his way back to the base alone.
Things didn't get much better when, two days later, he

crash-landed in front of British General John Higgins, commander of the air force. Higgins immediately ordered Bishop back to flight school for upgrading.

Major Alan Scott, the commanding officer of 60 Squadron, knew he could not afford to lose a single pilot—even one as bad as Bishop. He convinced the general to allow Bishop to stay for a few days until a replacement could be found. Bishop thanked the major by shooting down a German Albatros D.III the very next day. It was not a complete success, as Bishop's engine failed and he crash-landed in no-man's-land just 300 metres from the German lines.

After returning to the base on foot, Bishop was greeted by Higgins who reversed his order and allowed him to stay in France. Bishop was a quick learner, and on April 8 he scored his fifth victory, which made him an ace.

For the Royal Flying Corps, April 1917 became known as Bloody April. The 60 Squadron suffered a 110 percent casualty rate as 13 of the squadron's original 18 pilots, along with seven replacements, were shot down. On the other hand, April gave Bishop the chance to perfect his skills. Of the 35 confirmed kills by 60 Squadron that month, Bishop scored 12. On April 30 he even survived an encounter with Manfred von Richthofen, the Red Baron. According to Bishop's own account:

…I was up in the air again, with my squadron commander, to see if there were any Huns about looking for a bit of trouble…. Presently, to the south of us, we

saw five Albatross Scouts. We went after them, but before we had come within firing distance we discovered four red Albatrosses, just to our right. This latter quartet, I believe, was made up of Baron Von Richthofen and three of his best men….

In my turn I opened fire on the Baron, and in another halfminute found myself in the midst of what seemed to be a stampede of bloodthirsty animals.

Everywhere I turned smoking bullets were jumping at me; and although I got in two or three good bursts at the Baron's "red devil," I was rather bewildered for two or three minutes, as I could not see what was happening to the Major, and was not at all certain as to what was going to happen to me.

Around we went in cyclonic circles for several minutes, here a flash of the Hun machines, then a flash of silver as my squadron commander would whizz by. All the time I would be in the same mix-up myself, every now and then finding a red machine in front of me, and letting in a round or two of quick shots. I was glad the Germans were scarlet and we were silver. There was no need to hesitate about firing when the right color flitted by your nose.

It was a lightning fight, and I have never been in anything just like it. Firing one moment, you would have to concentrate all your mind and muscle on the next in doing a quick turn to avoid a collision….

…I saw up above me four more machines coming down to join in the fight. Being far inside the German lines, I at once decided they were additional Huns, so

I "zoomed" up and out of the fight to be free for a moment and have a look around. The moment I did this I saw the approaching machines were triplanes belonging to one of our naval squadrons, and they were coming up for all they were worth to help us against the Albatrosses. The latter, however, had had enough of the fight by now, and at the moment I "zoomed" they dived, and flew away toward the earth.

Bishop was constantly pressing for more flying time. He flew every mission assigned to him and then asked for, and received, permission to fly solo hunting missions deep behind enemy lines. It was not without risk. After one mission, Bishop's mechanic counted 210 bullet holes in the pilot's plane. As the number of enemy planes Bishop destroyed increased, so did his reputation. To the other pilots he was Billy—the clown in the Officer's Mess. To the enemy he was a deadly threat.

Unknown to Bishop, his commanding officer had recommended him for the Victoria Cross for prolonged gallantry, though he did not receive it. Still, Bishop was promoted to captain (and won the Military Cross) for his gallantry at Vimy Ridge in shooting down a German observation balloon. Even the enemy was noticing the Canadian in his blue-nosed aircraft. To them he was "Hell's Handmaiden," and they placed a bounty on his head.

Based on his success, Bishop was granted a brief leave in early May 1917. In England he received a hero's welcome, and when he heard that Captain

Albert Ball, the leading ace with 44 victories, had been killed on May 7, he vowed to become Britain's greatest ace. It was quite a boast, as at that point Bishop had only 19 kills to his credit.

After returning to France, Bishop was soon flying again. After scoring more victories throughout May, he soon turned his sights on a much larger target. On June 1 Bishop was in the Officer's Mess trying to convince his fellow flyers to attack a German aerodrome well behind enemy lines. They all thought the mission was too dangerous, but Major Alan Scott, the commanding officer, agreed to the flight—if Bishop could convince the others to go.

Bishop had no luck. At 3:00 AM on June 2, even as Bishop headed for his airplane, he tried to talk Deputy Flight Commander Willy Fry into going with him. Fry rolled over and went back to sleep. So at exactly 3:57 AM Bishop, alone, climbed into the air and headed for his primary target, an airfield near Cambrai. No enemy aircraft were in the area. Flying deep behind enemy lines, Bishop moved on in search of another target.

He opened the attack on the airdrome at Esnes by strafing and destroying six Albatros D.III scouts and one two-seater on the ground. Swinging around and returning to the aerodrome, Bishop engaged three German planes taking off to attack him. He destroyed two as they became airborne and the third in the air. Turning west toward the front lines, he evaded a German flying patrol searching for him and landed safely at Filescamp Farm, despite having sustained considerable damage to his aircraft during his 103-minute flight.

This time Bishop won his Victoria Cross. Upon receiving his VC in August 1917, it was pointed out that his was one of only two awarded during World War I that violated a key rule: To win the Victoria Cross, the action must be witnessed by an officer. The citation, published in the *London Gazette* on August 11, 1917, read:

For most conspicuous bravery, determination, and skill. Captain Bishop, who had been sent out to work independently, flew first of all to an enemy aerodrome; finding no machines about, he flew on to another aerodrome about three miles south-east, which was at least 12 miles the other side of the line. Seven machines, some with their engines running, were on the ground. He attacked these from about fifty feet, and a mechanic, who was starting one of the engines, was seen to fall. One of the machines got off the ground, but at a height of sixty feet, Captain Bishop fired fifteen rounds into it at very close range, and it crashed to the ground. A second machine got off the ground, into which he fired thirty rounds at 150 yards range, and it fell into a tree. Two more machines then rose from the aerodrome. One of these he engaged at a height of 1,000 feet, emptying the rest of his drum of ammunition. This machine crashed 300 yards from the aerodrome, after which Captain Bishop emptied a whole drum into the fourth hostile machine, and then flew back to his station. Four hostile scouts were about 1,000 feet above him for about a mile of his return journey, but they would not attack. His machine was very badly shot about by machine gun fire from the ground.

Bishop's raid was controversial. After the war his detractors pointed out that there was no record of an aerodrome at the location described by Bishop. However, German records show that a temporary aerodrome was established by the German Army at Esnes to assist with moving three flights of Jagdstaffel 2s. The types of German aircraft involved in the transfer closely matched those described by Bishop.

In July 1917, 60 Squadron and Bishop saw their success rate climb dramatically when the Royal Aircraft Factory S.E.5 biplanes were delivered. The S.E.5s were fast and powerful and provided the pilot with great overall visibility. Flying the nimble aircraft, Bishop surpassed Ball's record of 44 kills in August.

Billy Bishop was ordered home in the autumn of 1917. The government of Canada knew that the public needed a hero, and Bishop fit the bill perfectly. In April 1918, after a public relations tour to boost the war effort and promote bond sales, Bishop returned to England, was promoted to major and given command of No. 85 Squadron—the Flying Foxes.

The Flying Foxes were a new squadron, and Bishop was ordered to build it from the ground up, which included choosing all the pilots himself. On May 22 Bishop and his squadron were in Petit Synthe, France, test flying their S.E.5a Scout aircraft. Back in combat only two days later, Bishop soon regained his position as the leading Allied ace with a total of 59 downed enemy aircraft, including one flown by German ace Paul Billik.

Much to Bishop's disgust, the Canadian government ordered him home. The prime minister recognized that if Bishop, the war hero, was killed in France, it would do irreparable harm to morale across the country and severely damage the war effort. Bishop was ordered out of France by noon on June 19. In a final act of defiance, Bishop flew a solo flight that morning and added another five kills to his total: two Pfalz D.IIIa scouts, a German reconnaissance aircraft and two other scouts that collided in mid-air trying to avoid him.

On August 5, Bishop was promoted to lieutenant colonel and became the Officer Commanding Designate of the Canadian Air Force Section of the General Staff, Headquarters Overseas Military Forces of Canada. He was returning to England after a visit to Canada when the Armistice was declared. On December 31, 1918, war ace Billy Bishop was discharged from the Canadian Expeditionary Force with 72 kills to his credit.

CHAPTER FOURTEEN

Moreuil Wood, France
March 1918

WHEN CANADIANS ANSWERED THE CALL to war in 1914, they believed the fighting would be over before Christmas of that year. Little did they know that not until 1919 would a large number of soldiers finally return home.

For those who signed up, the cavalry was considered the elite force. Tales abounded regarding the dash and élan of these horse-mounted modern knights, and anecdotes were told of heroic cavalry charges with sword and lance. But the mud of Flanders and the trenches of the Western Front mean that the cavalry saw few charges and much tedious waiting for their day of glory. In fact, Canadian cavalry glory did not come until March 30, 1918, at a place called Moreuil Wood.

In the fall of 1917, Field Marshall Sir Douglas Haig faced the very real possibility of defeat on the fields of Europe. The German Army of General Erich Ludendorff seemed to have all the advantages. The French Army was in near mutiny, the Russian Front had collapsed (potentially freeing up to one million men to fight on the Western Front) and the government in the United Kingdom was internally divided. Consequently, Haig, believing the best defence was a good offence, attacked at Passchendaele in October. While it was a victory on paper, taking the small Flanders town made little difference to the outcome of the war.

By early 1918 the tables had turned completely. It was Ludendorff's turn to take the offensive. His reality was that morale in the German Army was collapsing. The American Army, with one million fresh soldiers, was starting to arrive in Europe. At home in Germany, support for the war was waning. For Ludendorff, victory in Europe was a necessity, and this might be his last opportunity.

At 4:00 AM on March 21, 1918, Ludendorff threw three full armies against the weakest part of the Allied lines as part of Operation Michael. In the face of the German onslaught, the Allied 3rd Cavalry Division, along with 200 men and horses from the Canadian Cavalry Brigade, were ordered to Bouchoire to try to hold back the waves of German infantry. They failed, and the Germans soon penetrated as far as 45 kilometres behind the Allied front lines.

However, Ludendorff's armies were victims of their own success. By travelling so far so fast, his armies outran their ability to resupply the attacking troops on the front lines. The general ordered a halt to the advance so the gains could be consolidated and supply lines strengthened. But by the time the German attack was resumed on March 30, the Allies had gathered themselves and were ready for what was to come.

For the men of the Canadian Cavalry Brigade, it seemed that Operation Michael would again offer little opportunity for the horsemen to be of use. Cavalry's role was to chase down enemy infantry once the Allied infantry had broken both their line and their fighting spirit. Once Operation Michael ground to a halt, few cavalrymen thought they would be required. Instead it seemed likely they would return to the rear to wait for the long-anticipated breakthrough.

However, the Allied high command realized the importance of stopping the Germans from advancing any farther. During the lull that followed the German's initial advance, various elements of the Canadian Cavalry Brigade were ordered to the River Avre opposite Moreuil Wood and nearby Rifle Wood.

As Operation Michael resumed on the morning of March 30, the German 23rd Saxon Division was in full control of Moreuil Wood. The small forest overlooked the Avre River and, of greater importance to the Allies, it controlled the Amiens-Paris Railway.

At Moreuil Wood that day were the Lord Strathcona's Horse and the Royal Canadian Dragoons. At full strength, a cavalry squadron consisted of 150 men and officers. Within the squadron were four troops, each led by a lieutenant. In total, with all of the required support staff, a cavalry regiment was supposed to have 18 officers and 503 men. Because of the heavy fighting undertaken as dismounted infantrymen during the preceding weeks, the Lord Strathcona's Horse had only 373 men; the Royal Canadian Dragoons had about the same.

At 8:30 AM British General J.E.B. "Jack" Seely approached Moreuil Wood with orders to take the area if the opportunity arose but to do as much as possible to delay the German advance. By 9:30 he was close enough to the Germans occupying the wood that he came under enemy rifle fire. An attempt to take Moreuil Wood had to be made, and it was to be the Canadians leading the charge. Seely ordered the Canadians to cross the Avre River, enter Moreuil Wood and come around the German defenders. The wood itself was triangular in shape, its ash trees not yet in leaf. Each side of the triangle was approximately two kilometres in length and presented a formidable obstacle to the mounted Canadians. Seely explained his plans.

The Royal Canadian Dragoons are to send one squadron to the right of the Bois de Moreuil, occupy the southeast corner and get in touch with the French in the village of Moreuil. The other two squadrons are to gallop around the left face of the wood and endeavour to seize the northeast corner of it. Lord Strathcona's Horse are to follow close behind these two squadrons of Dragoons and send one squadron forward to gallop right around the northeast corner, engage the Germans who are entering the wood by mounted attack and, having dispersed them, occupy the southeast face of the wood. The remaining two squadrons of Strathcona's are to enter the wood just beyond my headquarters at the southern point, fight their way through, and join their comrades on the eastern face. Fort Garry's are to be in reserve with me.

Seely headed across the river for Moreuil Wood with Royal Canadian Dragoons, the Strathcona's Horse, the Machine Gun Squadron and the Fort Garry Horse close behind. As the Canadians neared the wood, they came under intense rifle and machine-gun fire. A squadron of the Royal Canadian Dragoons pressed home the attack. Captain Roy Nordheimer of the Dragoons, later wrote that:

> *The first troop, under Lieutenant Cochran, galloped into the wood, but they were soon driven out by heavy machine gun fire. I ordered the squadron to dismount, and reentered the wood with bayonets fixed and Hotchkiss guns supporting our flanks. We drove the enemy out of the part of the wood which we faced and occupied the edge.*

The fighting broke down to vicious hand-to-hand combat using swords and pistols. Ultimately the Germans were driven deeper into the wood.

Recognizing the difficulties the Dragons were facing, the Strathconas immediately deployed around the wood. C Squadron was assigned to cut off any German reinforcements entering the woods from the northeast. A and B Squadrons dismounted and attacked on foot from the north. At the same time, patrols were sent forward to scout the enemy's positions.

Lieutenant Gordon Flowerdew, C Squadron's commanding officer, ordered Lieutenant Frederick Harvey to take his men ahead as an advance party. Two hundred metres from the northeast corner of the wood, Harvey encountered German soldiers looting a supply wagon. He ordered shots fired, and the Germans were killed. Almost immediately Harvey and his men came under fire from inside Moreuil Wood. He quickly ordered his men to dismount and start into the wood. At that moment, Flowerdew rode up, and the two lieutenants hastily devised a plan. Harvey would continue to press forward, while Flowerdew took the mounted soldiers of C Squadron to the end of the woods to cut off any escaping Germans—the classic role of mounted cavalry.

In the meantime, A and B Squadrons of the Strathconas halted about 900 metres from the northern edge of the woods. In the face of intense German fire, the Strathcona's B Squadron dismounted and proceeded into the wood, while A and C Squadrons of the Fort Garry Horse attacked from the west. Providing cover fire for the six cavalry squadrons now in Moreuil Wood was B Squadron of the Fort Garry Horse, which had gained some high ground in the woods across the Avre River. From this vantage point they poured rifle and machine-gun fire into the German positions.

From the air the Royal Flying Corps (RFC) was also battering the enemy. As the 243rd German Division marched toward Moreuil Wood to relieve the besieged 23 Saxon Division, they came under aerial attack. German reports recorded that, "dense marching columns attracted numerous enemy air units which attacked with bombs and machine guns.... With improved weather and good visibility numerous enemy planes were constantly attacking and without hindrance circling above our positions...the enemy planes were attacking more boldly."

At Moreuil Wood the German defenders were shown little mercy by the RFC pilots, who dropped 109 bombs on the German positions and strafed ground troops with 17,000 machine-gun rounds.

At the northeast corner of the wood, Flowerdew had just reached his agreed-to position when he saw a group of more than 300 Germans trying to withdraw, taking a howitzer and several machine guns with them. For Flowerdew it was the classic situation for which he had been trained—escaping infantry taking guns with them.

Yelling, "It's a charge boys, it's a charge!" Flowerdew spurred his horse forward. Trumpeter Reg Longley tried to sound the charge but was shot from his saddle before playing a single note. C Squadron crashed into the German lines. Cavalry troopers slashed with swords, cutting their way through the enemy mass. Once through the German infantry, they wheeled around to face the woods. In front of them, on the other side of the enemy, Flowerdew could see Harvey and his men emerging from the woods. The Canadians charged again, trying to get through to Harvey.

Private Albert Dale of 4th Troop later wrote that everything seemed unreal, "the shouting of men, the moans of the wounded, the pitiful crying of the wounded and dying horses...." Sergeant Tom MacKay suffered 59 wounds to one leg alone. Casualties throughout the squadron were heavy.

Flowerdew was shot from his horse, mortally wounded in the chest and leg; Harvey and another man tried to drag Flowerdew to the relative safety of the woods. Private Harry Hooker raced to General Seeley and informed him that C Squadron had been completely destroyed in the charge.

After the fact it was hard to determine exactly how many men participated in C Squadron's charge, but it was later estimated that 75 Canadians attacked the 300 withdrawing German infantrymen. It is known that 24 Canadians were killed, leaving only 51 survivors. From this group, 15 more died from their wounds during the next few weeks. It had been a cavalry charge, but it was far from glorious.

By 11:00 AM only the extreme southern end of the woods was still controlled by the Germans. When Allied reinforcements began to arrive, Seely ordered Moreuil Wood cleared of all pockets of resistance. As the troops worked their way through the woods, Allied artillery continued to rain shells into the wood. With no enemy present, the British and Canadians troops were in danger of being killed by friendly fire. Only after repeated calls to the artillery positions did the message got through—the guns went silent. Casualties were cared for, ammunition resupplied and defences prepared.

The Canadian Cavalry Brigade suffered 305 casualties. According to one historian,

The Dragoons lost one officer, 19 other ranks killed, three officers and 48 other ranks wounded and 22 missing.

The Fort Garry Horse had one killed, one officer and 36 other ranks wounded and three missing. In the Strathcona's A Squadron had nine killed, B Squadron eleven, Signal Troop one, and C Squadron 24, for a total of 45; 120 were wounded. The Machine Gun Squadron had eight wounded and the Field Ambulance one.

However, Moreuil Wood was in Allied hands.

All that changed the next morning. On March 31 the Germans counterattacked and recaptured most of Moreuil Wood and all of Rifle Wood. The next day the 2nd Cavalry Division was ordered to retake the Wood. Seely called on the 4th Cavalry Brigade to push north toward Hangard, while the 5th Cavalry Brigade was to seize the northeast edge of the Wood. Once this objective was reached, the Canadians were to bypass the 5th Cavalry and recapture the woods.

By 11:00 AM the Canadians were back in control of Rifle Wood. This battle was decided at a cost of another 175 Canadian casualties. But by April 5 both Moreuil Wood and Rifle Wood were back in German hands. They kept control of both woods until the Battle of Amiens in August 1918.

On April 5, General Ludendorff called off Operation Michael. His push to victory had stalled after costing him 250,000 killed, wounded or missing—losses he could not replace. Making matters worse for the German war effort, American troops were flooding into Europe. The end of Operation Michael was the beginning of the end of German aspirations in Europe.

CHAPTER FIFTEEN

Amiens, France
August 1918

AFTER CANADIAN SUCCESS AT VIMY RIDGE and Hill 70, where enemy positions were taken by the Canadians against heavy odds, the enemy named the Canadians "storm troopers" for, according to the German infantry, "We can stop the British and we can stop the Australians but we cannot stop the Canadians—they come on like a storm." Nowhere was this truer than at Amiens in northern France.

Sir Arthur Currie, Commander in Chief of the Canadian Corps, recalled that in early 1918 the Allies were in serious trouble all along the Western Front.

> (The Boche) attacked us with great success. They penetrated deeply into our lines and almost separated the British army from the French. Shortly after that, they attacked again just south of Arras in early April. They attacked again north of La Bassee and again bulged our line, and the only part of the British front that did not give was the part held by the Canadian Corps.

By the late spring of 1918, it was clear that the German offensive "Operation Michael" had failed, and Allied Generalissimo Ferdinand Foch ordered a counteroffensive. The Allies had finally gained

numerical superiority over the Germans, as each
month another 250,000 American troops entered
the European Theatre.

At the Battle of Hamel on July 4, the Australians
quickly overwhelmed well-entrenched troops using
surprise and a creeping artillery barrage timed to the
attack by the infantry, rather than the usual massive
artillery barrage prior to the attack. Based on the
Australians' success, British general Henry Rawlinson
finalized a plan of attack and told Brigadier General
Currie on July 20 that the Canadian Corps was to
attack and free the Paris-Amiens railway. The date for
the attack was set for August 8, 1918.

General headquarters ordered that, "It is of the
first importance that secrecy should be observed and
the operation carried out as a surprise." In an effort
to mislead German observers, the boundary between
the British Fourth Army and the French First Army
was moved 6400 metres south. The British III Corps
took over the Australian positions north of the
Somme, and the Australians stretched their positions
to cover the gaps. To the Germans, it appeared the
Allies were weakening their front rather than rein-
forcing it for an attack.

Currie started moving Canadian troops from Arras
to the Amiens region on July 30. The men were
loaded onto trains and buses and were told that they
were going to Ypres to reinforce the Second Army.
Pasted inside the cover of every Canadian's pay book
was the order "KEEP YOUR MOUTH SHUT" that

cautioned against discussing any part of the plan, and, if taken prisoner, from giving the enemy anything more than name and rank. According to the order: "Though the enemy might use threats, he will respect you if your courage, patriotism, and self-control do not fail."

All of the preparations were put at risk in the early hours of August 4 when a German raiding party captured five soldiers from the 4th Australian Division. All activity on the Canadian side of the front line ground to a halt as fears of a security breach spread. The original plan was for the Canadians to be fully in place on the night of August 6–7. In fact, the Canadians did not finally move up until just hours before the attack was to begin.

The French First Army had seven divisions covering a front that stretched more than six kilometres on either side of Moreuil. Three Canadian divisions were placed south of the Roye road extending to just north of the railway to Chaulnes; between the railway and the Ancre River were two divisions of the Australian Corps and three of the British III Corps. In immediate reserve were three French, one Canadian and two Australian divisions—for a total of 21 Allied divisions.

As the hours counted down, Rawlinson ordered his commanders to move as quickly as possible to the Roye-Chaulnes road, another 13 kilometres farther on. If all the objectives were achieved, the British would recapture all the territory they had occupied in the spring of 1917 (and had subsequently lost). Rawlinson pointed out that it would be even better if they could push on to Ham, 21 kilometres beyond Chaulnes, to assist the French.

In past battles, artillery barrages had alerted the enemy to the impending infantry attacks. At Amiens, the surprise was total. At 12 minutes before zero hour, as a thick ground fog drifted over the battle-field, tanks that were staging 900 metres behind the front began to lumber forward. An Allied bomber roared low overhead, and the normal harassing fire provided by the artillery covered their noise. According to Captain R.J. Renison:

At 4:20 to the moment a blaze of crimson lighted the whole horizon behind us for miles. Three seconds later, there was a deafening roar from hundreds of guns. The enemy's noise was instantly lost in the din—the shells screamed overhead like countless legions of destroying angels. In front the green turf was churned by an invisible harrow. It was impossible to distin-guish the sound of the individual guns, but rather the concussion resembled the throbbing of an engine built to drive a planet on its course.

With one accord along the whole line, the men leaped on the parapet and went "over the top." The company officers with synchronised watches and compasses, led their men as if on parade…. One unit was led over by its pipe band. In another place, the Tank "Dominion" led the procession with a piper skirling from its top. The tanks looked like prehistoric monsters as they lumbered

over the trenches into the mist with their noses to the
ground on the trail of the machine-gun nests.

To reduce casualties, Rawlinson ordered the troops to attack in five distinct waves separated by intervals of 90 metres. The first two waves were made up of skirmishers who helped guide the tanks. Behind them were section columns in single file, and last up were the carrying parties bringing supplies to the front. To ensure the infantry could keep up with the tanks, Rawlinson ordered them to carry only what was needed. Overhead, the No. 5 (Corps Reconnaissance) Squadron RAF provided air support to the Canadians, while other air squadrons were active all along the line. Surprise was so complete that it took the German defenders at least five minutes to register that a major offensive was underway and to open fire with their artillery. By then the German guns were shelling empty fields as the attackers had long since moved forward.

As the Canadian Corps moved though the Luce Valley, it faced heavy fighting at the Hangard Cemetery, which knocked out 11 of its original tanks. The 1st Canadian Division captured Aubercourt but encountered stiff resistance at Hangard Wood. As the division pushed on, the enemy at Morgemont Wood finally broke and retreated in disorder. By 11:00 AM the 1st Division was in Cayeux.

Meanwhile, the 2nd Canadian Division quickly captured Marcelcave and entered Wiencourt by 9:20 AM, losing only four of their tanks in the process. By noon the Canadians had outrun their artillery cover, but it mattered little. Few of the German guns were still firing, and men and equipment were being moved forward en masse through the Santerre plateau.

Soon the Canadian Cavalry Brigade, moving up to cover the Amiens–Roye road, captured Beaucourt. As they dealt with resistance at Le Quesnel, other Canadian units entered Cayeux and moved beyond to Caix and Guillaucourt. The 4th Canadian Division, which had been held in reserve, was ordered forward and passed through the original attacking divisions. By the evening of August 8, only Le Quesnel was not in Canadian control.

Rawlinson's plan called for the third phase of the battle to be handled by Mark V tanks. However, the German defences were crumbling so quickly that the infantry broke through without the assistance of the tanks. The cavalry, waiting since 1914 to have a real role to play in a war dominated by static trench warfare, took up the offensive. One cavalry brigade in the Australian sector and two in the Canadian, combined with RAF bombing and armoured-car fire, prevented the Germans from regrouping. By 3:00 PM the Allies were already holding 2000 prisoners in a single wire cage. Before nightfall the Germans realized that the Allies had opened a gap 24-kilometres wide in the German lines south of the Somme.

The success of the Allied offensive at Amiens handed Germany its greatest loss since the beginning of the war. For the Allies, the gains made during a single day were impressive and the losses comparatively light. The Canadians drove the Germans back 13 kilometres, and the Australians gained 11 kilometres. The French and British found the going tougher, but on the flanks the French advanced eight kilometres and the British three. Total losses to the Fourth Army were 8800 casualties.

Official German figures gave their Second Army's casualties as, "650 to 700 officers and 26,000 to 27,000 other ranks with approximately 13,000 of those prisoners. Allied forces had destroyed or seized more than 400 guns, many trench mortars and a 'huge number of machine-guns.'" In their attacks, the Allies completely overran five German divisions. German Army Chief of Staff Paul von Hindenburg later commented that counterattacks, which were so important to German strategy, had become impossible when command positions became isolated by Allied attacks.

"August 8th," General Erich Ludendorff wrote, was, "der Schwarzer Tag des deutschen Heeres" (the black day of the German Army). For the Germans it was the beginning of the end of the war. "Everything I had feared, and of which I had so often given warning," Ludendorff declared pessimistically, "had here, in one place, become a reality."

Colonel G.W.L. Nicholson, author of *The Official History of the Canadian Army in the First World War: Canadian Expeditionary Force, 1914-1919,* noted, "No longer could he [Ludendorff] hope to resume the offensive or find any strategic expedient in which German forces might be employed to advantage. Even the Kaiser was now convinced that as a result of the failure of the German July offensive and the defeat on 8 August the war could no longer be won."

CHAPTER SIXTEEN

Siberia
1918–1919

FOR MOST CANADIANS, WORLD WAR I ended with the signing of the armistice in France on November 11, 1918. Few knew or cared that Canadian soldiers were a world away in Siberia, helping the White Russians resist the Bolshevik Revolution.

For the Allies, 1917 had been disastrous on the Eastern Front. A March revolution overthrew Russian Czar Nicholas II. While unsuccessful in establishing a real government, this action sparked a massive mutiny in the Russian Army that eliminated any real resistance to the German Army. In March 1918, Germany and Russia signed a peace agreement at Brest-Litovsk. The agreement raised the very real spectre of one million German soldiers being released to fight on the Western Front.

The Allies, including Canada, were not ready to recognize the new Bolshevik government in Russia. As a resistance movement called the White Russians developed along the Don River in Northern Russia, the Allies saw the chance to re-open an Eastern Front. When the Japanese, who ultimately led the intervention in Siberia, arrived in Vladivostok in January 1918, they found transportation problems had stranded 660,000 tonnes of war material sent by the Allies and meant for the resistance. Two days after the Japanese arrived, the British cruiser HMS *Suffolk* dropped anchor in Vladivostok's Golden Horn Bay and started preparations for the coming campaign.

By May 1918, the Czecho-Slovak Legion had captured 6000 kilometres of the Trans-Siberian Railway (from the Ural Mountains to Vladivostok) from the Red Army. The Legion, an "army without a country," comprised 66,000 former prisoners of war who saw the Russian Revolution as a chance to establish an independent country for themselves. For the Allies, the Czecho-Slovak Legion was the perfect "shock troops" in their efforts to dislodge the Bolsheviks.

On June 28, 1918, the Allies, along with the Czecho-Slovak Legion, were ready to strike. The Legion, supported by marines from the Japanese, American, British and Chinese ships anchored in Golden Horn Bay, quickly gained control of the railway station, arms depot and other strategic points across Vladivostok. The local (Soviet) government was soon ousted from power, leaving the White Government in control.

The turn of events in Siberia gave the Allies hope that things on the Eastern Front were changing for the better. Canadian Prime Minister Sir Robert Borden, in concert with other Allied leaders, endorsed a plan to send troops to Murmansk, Arkhangelsk (Archangel) and the Caspian Sea in an effort to encircle and defeat the Red Army. Borden showed his support by pledging Canadian troops to the campaign.

Returning to Canada from England, Borden addressed the Privy Council on August 12 and argued for a Canadian Siberian Expedition Force (CSEF) made up of 4000 troops. But Canada's generals in France weighed into the debate. Borden agreed to their demands that the Siberian force be all volunteer, so that regular recruiting efforts would not be affected. On August 23, 1918, an Order in Council officially established the CSEF.

The British and Canadian governments agreed that Canada's efforts should be bolstered by 1500 British troops. For the first time, a Canadian, Major General James H. Elmsley, named to command the CSEF, would lead British troops in the field. He officially reported to Japanese Lieutenant General Keijiro Otani, Commander in Chief of all Allied troops in the Russian maritime provinces, but he had a separate reporting line directly back to Prime Minister Borden. The Canadian Army had come a long way from 1914, when the British High Command considered Canadian soldiers suitable only as replacements to fill in British ranks.

As Elmsley prepared his contingent for Siberia, United States President Wilson authorized a deployment of troops to officially "assist the Czecho-Slovak Legion in its efforts to escape Russian repression." Wilson wanted no part of an invasion, but assisting a resistance group could be sold to Congress and the American people.

Elmsley soon found recruiting an all-volunteer force impossible. Men returning from the Western Front saw little attraction in heading off to war again—this time in an even colder and more inhospitable part of the world. Headquarters staff was soon using conscripts to supplement the force. Ultimately, the CSEF consisted of two infantry battalions (the 259th and 260th Canadian Rifles), two batteries of artillery, a machine-gun company and a squadron of Royal Northwest Mounted Police. The balance of the force was assigned either to headquarters or support roles.

Throughout the autumn of 1918, the CSEF gathered in Vancouver and trained for the intervention in Siberia. The first 706 Canadian troops, led by General Elmsley and his advance party, consisted of headquarters staff, support elements for administration, medical support, and logistics and food preparation staff. They boarded the CPR ship *Empress of Japan* and cast off on October 11, and arrived in Vladivostok 15 days later.

The Canadian troops were soon living in an old Russian army barracks, while General Elmsley established his headquarters in the ornate Pushkinskaya Theatre. Elmsley quickly learned that the Allies were struggling to stabilize conditions in Siberia. The situation on the ground was hardly a surprise. The chief of defence staff had warned Borden that logistics lacked "co-ordination and control," that the Trans-Siberian Railway was "seriously disorganized" and that there was "no general agreement" among the Allies.

Furthermore, the White Russian Army was contending with internal power struggles even as soldiers from White Russian, Czecho-Slovak, French and Polish units battled the Red Army in the Ural Mountains. In November 1918 the Red-led provisional government in Omsk, the capital city of Siberia, fell to Admiral Aleksandr Kolchak, the former commander of the Czar's Black Sea Fleet who crowned himself "Supreme Ruler of All Russia."

Elmsley dispatched 55 Canadians to Omsk to support the British troops there. A further 200 Canadian soldiers assisted Japanese, Czecho-Slovak, Italian and Chinese troops repulse an attack by Red Army partisans who attacked the village of Shkotovo, just north of Vladivostok, and threatened the city's coal supply and ultimately the Trans-Siberian Railway.

Partisan activity in the Vladivostok region was growing. The partisan leader at Shkotovo sent a message to the Allied command saying, "We declare a fight to the death. Just as the Allied troops left Odessa and Arkhangelsk, so also you will be forced to leave Vladivostok." Men from Shkotovo were operating throughout the Vladivostok area disrupting lines of communications, blowing up bridges, seizing towns and destroying sections of the Trans-Siberian Railway.

Within weeks of the Canadians arriving in Siberia, and just as Kolchak consolidated his power, the armistice was declared in Europe. However, because the stated intention of the expedition was to assist the Czecho-Slovak Legion, many of the Allies were unwilling to end the fight. They saw a role for the assembled army and committed the troops to continue fighting the Red Army into 1919.

In the days before satellite communications, events often overtook the decisions being made in both Siberia and Ottawa. At home, opposition to the Siberian Expedition was growing. Farm and labour groups were protesting Canada's participationin the war, and the Borden government was feeling politically threatened.

Prime Minster Borden was in Europe at the peace talks, and the cabinet in Ottawa was being directed by acting Prime Minister Sir Thomas White. White sent a telegram to Borden advising him that, "public opinion here will not sustain us in continuing to send troops, many of whom are draftees under the Military Service Act and Order in Council, now that the war is ended." For the British and Canadians, the decision was simple: their troops should be brought home as quickly as militarily possible. Just as the bulk of the Canadian troops arrived in Vladivostok in January 1919, the government decided to withdraw the CSEF without it ever seeing direct action.

So from January onward, the Canadian troops spent their time doing what all soldiers do—guard duty, polishing boots and equipment, and playing sports, including hockey, soccer and baseball. Headquarters supported the establishment of two brigade newspapers: *The Siberian Bugle* and *Siberian Sapper.*

When they weren't visiting the officially sanctioned movie theatres and canteen huts, the soldiers found Vladivostok to be a siren song. The city was an international centre with sailors and soldiers from a multitude of countries. For the Canadian troops, the Chinese bazaar, Russian baths and brothels were a welcome distraction.

However, by the spring of 1919, soldiers were no longer allowed into the city, and anyone leaving the barracks had to be armed. Soon partisans were operating within Vladivostok itself, sabotaging Allied military equipment and even killing White Russian and Allied officers. Ottawa determined that it was time for Canadian soldiers to come home.

Altogether 19 Canadians were killed in Siberia, and on June 1, 1919, a monument was erected in their memory overlooking the sea at the Marine Cemetery on the Churkin Peninsula. Elmsley and his remaining staff boarded the *Monteagle* on June 5 and sailed east for Victoria. Canada's intervention in Siberia was over. By all accounts, it was a failure.

In Siberia, the White Russian government lasted only another seven months, to be replaced by a Soviet government that remained in control for 70 years. At home in Canada, Borden's government also paid a price for the Siberian Expedition. In 1921, Arthur Meighen, who replaced Borden when he retired in 1920, was voted out of office in Canada's first post-war election.

CANADIAN BATTLES

World War II

CHAPTER SEVENTEEN

Hong Kong
December 1941

FEW CANADIANS KNOW THAT CANADA's first battle of World War II was not on a field in Europe but on an island in Asia. Canada's initial taste of the conflict to come involved defending the British Crown Colony of Hong Kong against the attacking Japanese in December 1941. The cost was very high.

For the British, Hong Kong was a difficult problem. The small island colony, tucked into the coast of China, became a valuable piece of real estate—at least in a military sense—with the expansion of the Sino-Japanese War. Faced with the Japanese threat, the British initially considered Hong Kong expendable. It was decided not to send reinforcements but rather to save them for another fight. In October 1938, when the Japanese captured Canton (now Guangzhou), about 120 kilometres northwest of Hong Kong, the British outpost was effectively surrounded. It was considered impossible to defend, despite the work undertaken to harden the island's defences, which included construction of the Gin Drinkers Line, a series of fortifications on the Kowloon Peninsula.

In September 1941, British Prime Minister Winston Churchill reversed the no-reinforcements decision, believing that a show of force might deter the Japanese from further moves against China. Hong Kong was to become a bastion. Shortly thereafter, the Canadian government offered the British two infantry battalions and a brigade headquarters to assist in the defence of the island.

In October, the Royal Rifles of Canada and the Winnipeg Grenadiers, under the command of Brigadier J.K. Lawson, were ordered to Hong Kong. Designated C Force, the men arrived on the troopship *Awatea* on November 16 without their vehicles, which had been diverted to the Philippines. Few of the Canadians had any military experience. It didn't seem to matter, as most didn't believe they would see any real combat. After all, it was thought that the Japanese were busy enough elsewhere.

Indeed, the Japanese high command launched a series of lightning strikes against Pearl Harbor, northern Malaya, the Philippines, Guam and Wake Island. But less than eight hours after the attack on Pearl Harbor, the 38th Division of the Japanese Imperial Army struck Hong Kong. Led by Lieutenant General Takashi Sakai, an experienced Japanese army of 52,000 men faced a combined force of 14,000 British, Canadian and Indian forces, supported by a small group of Hong Kong volunteers, and led by Major General Christopher Michael Maltby.

The Japanese quickly established air superiority by bombing Kai Tak Airport and destroying two Vickers Vildebeest torpedo-reconnaissance aircraft and two Supermarine Walrus amphibious planes. With their planes gone, the ground and aircrews from the Royal Air Force station volunteered to fight as infantrymen. Meanwhile, British warships, vulnerable without air support, were ordered to sail from Hong Kong to Singapore.

In the face of vastly superior Japanese forces, the defenders quickly decided not to hold the Sham Chun River. Instead, three battalions were moved to the Gin Drinkers Line in the hills above the city. They had little effect. On December 10 the Japanese broke through at the Shing Mun redoubt, forcing the evacuation of Kowloon the next day under heavy enemy artillery fire. As the last defenders left Kowloon for Hong Kong Island on December 13, they destroyed or sabotaged as many military facilities as possible—leaving little behind for the enemy.

On the same day, Maltby split his forces into an East Brigade and a West Brigade and was immediately faced with a demand from the Japanese to surrender. Maltby refused, and Japanese began bombing the north shore of the island. On December 17 another demand to surrender was forwarded to the Allied headquarters. Again it was rejected, so Sakai prepared his ground troops for an invasion of Hong Kong.

When the Japanese landed at North Point (in the northeast of the island) during the evening of December 18, they suffered only light casualties because an effective defence could not be mounted until daybreak when the enemy could be seen by the defenders. The tone for the coming battle was set when the Japanese tortured and killed 20 Allied gunners from the Sai Wan Battery—after they had surrendered.

The Royal Rifles and the Winnipeg Grenadiers, along with their allies, soon found themselves engaged in battles across the island, battles that often deteriorated into hand-to-hand combat. Despite often-heroic efforts by the defenders, the Japanese rapidly destroyed the West Brigade Headquarters and secured a position in the Wong Nai Chung Gap that controlled all movement between the city and southern parts of the island.

By December 20 the Japanese had spilt Hong Kong in two, with British forces controlling Stanley Peninsula and the western part of the island. All else, including the island's water reservoirs, were in Japanese hands. Everyone knew it was just a matter of time before the Allies would be forced to surrender.

During the morning of December 25, the final day of the Battle of Hong Kong, Japanese troops entered the British Field Hospital at St. Stephan's College and tortured and killed 60 injured soldiers along with their doctors and other staff. For both the military and Sir Mark Aitchison Young, the Governor of Hong

Kong, it was time to surrender the colony. For the residents of Hong Kong, this date became known as Black Christmas.

The garrison had held out for 17 days. For the Canadians the cost was high—290 killed and 493 wounded. Many more soldiers died during the next three and a half years, as the Canadian prisoners of war endured terrible conditions at Japanese forced labour camps. Barely existing on 800 calories a day, the soldiers worked in coalmines and shipyards, and many died from exposure and disease. Of the 1975 Canadians who boarded the *Awatea*, 550 died in Hong Kong or Japan.

CHAPTER EIGHTEEN

Dieppe Raid
August 1942

FOR CANADIANS, MANY BATTLES RESONATE: Vimy Ridge for forging a nation, Passchendaele for the horror of the mud, and Amiens for signalling the end of World War I. In World War II, the raid on Dieppe resonated not because of victory but because of failure. To Canadians, the loss of life and the failure to achieve even a single objective made Dieppe appear to be a costly and unnecessary battle—and a colossal error. In fact the raid on Dieppe, or Operation Jubilee as it was officially known, was not the poorly planned raid on Europe that it seemed.

When the British Expeditionary Force was evacuated from Europe at Dunkirk in late May 1940, it became clear that a large amphibious force would be required if the Allies were to successfully re-establish a presence on the continent. Immediately after Dunkirk, a Combined Operations Headquarters was established to develop the tools, techniques and strategies needed for an amphibious attack on German defences along the coast of France. As early as 1941, the Allies had a plan for landing 12 divisions on the coast of France near Le Havre. But the attack could not take place unless Germany moved large numbers of troops to the Russian Front.

When the hoped-for movement of German troops to Russia did not occur, the Allies again faced the problem of how to establish a beachhead in Europe. The questions were legion. Could a large port be taken and held by an amphibious force? Would the new landing craft be up to the task? Could the air force be used to support the attacking ground troops without destroying the port itself? Could the navy, air force and army actually work in a coordinated and cohesive way? Most important, could the element of surprise be maintained?

Recognizing that the only way to get the answers was to stage an actual raid on a fortified port, Combined Operations Headquarters began to plan Operation Rutter. Their timing could not have been better. Joseph Stalin, Russia's leader, had appealed to British Prime Minister Churchill and U.S. President Eisenhower to open a second front. The Russian people were enduring repeated, vicious attacks by the German Army. They needed relief, and a raid on France would, it was believed, distract the Germans and cause them to pull vital resources out of Russia.

While many options were put forward, it was finally decided that Operation Rutter would involve an amphibious attack against Dieppe, a resort town in Normandy. Perched on a cliff facing the English Channel, the town would be no easy conquest. The

Germans had fortified the area and installed artillery batteries at nearby Berneval and Varengeville.

The final version of the plan called for a June 1942 attack by land, sea and air force elements. If all went well, RAF Spitfires and Hurricanes would fly more than 1000 sorties directly from Sussex to weaken the German defenders. Naval bombardment would further prepare the way for attacks by infantry on the town and both flanks.

When it became clear that the attack was real, the Canadians clamoured for the opportunity to lead the raid. Swayed by the Canadian argument that they had been inactive too long, Churchill ordered Operation Rutter to go ahead, with the Canadians making up the bulk of the force.

On July 5, 1942, the 2nd Canadian Division boarded the 250 ships that would take them to France. But the day before the flotilla was to weigh anchor, they were discovered and attacked by a group of German bombers. With all hope of surprise now gone, Operation Rutter was called off, and a raid on Dieppe seemed to have slipped away.

While many in the Allied headquarters wanted to permanently cancel the raid, the new Chief of Combined Operations—Louis Mountbatten—did not. Renaming Rutter as Operation Jubilee, he devised a new plan without getting approval from the Combined Chiefs of Staff. Mountbatten effectively cut himself off from any assistance from headquarters, including sources of new and vital intelligence.

Mountbatten's plan called for assault troops to land on the beach at daybreak and move to the flanks, with the objective of destroying the artillery at Berneval and Varengeville. This would permit a direct assault on the town a half hour later. Normally, the attackers could count on bombers softening up a target before they went in. Mountbatten's plan required complete surprise; there would be no covering bombers to protect the ground troops. Once the harbour and German landing barges were captured, the troops were to destroy vital German installations and be back on the ships to return to England at high tide. After all, Jubilee was a raid, not an invasion.

Once again the Canadians were chosen for the raid. Canadian General Andrew McNaughton, Commander of the First Canadian Infantry Division, was concerned that the Canadians had been in Europe for almost two years and had yet to participate in a major operation. At home, the Canadian media and the public were questioning why the Canadians were not seeing action. McNaughton believed the Dieppe raid would give his soldiers the training they needed, and the folks at home the action they desired.

Altogether, 4963 men and officers from the 2nd Canadian Division, 1005 British commandos, 50 U.S. rangers and 15 French soldiers were to hit the beach at Dieppe. They would disembark from 237 ships and landing barges, including six destroyers. The new Landing Craft Tanks would disgorge 29 Churchill tanks, three outfitted with flamethrowers. The Churchills, adapted for running through shallow water after unloading, would provide rolling protection and firepower for the infantrymen.

While no bombers would fly on the night before the assault, on the day of the attack, the soldiers would get air support from the fighters and bombers of the Royal Air Force and Royal Canadian Air Force. In the air, the Allies had a numerical advantage over the defenders, but the Spitfires and Hurricanes could stay over their targets for only a short period of time as they would be operating at maximum range. The Germans were flying from bases much closed to the action and would be able to stay in the battle for much longer.

Waiting for the Canadians and their allies were about 1500 German soldiers spread across the cliffs and in neighbouring towns. Only 150 defenders were actually on the beach at Dieppe, with even fewer manning the approaches to the town. Other troops were in position to defend the artillery batteries on either flank. The stage was set for the raid on Dieppe.

During the night of August 18, 1942, 252 ships departed for France. If Mountbatten's plan for surprise was to succeed, the men had to be on the beach before dawn.

Under cover of darkness, No. 4 British Commando was the first to reach its objective. After successfully landing on Orange Beach on the extreme right flank of the attack, the men charged up a steep slope and captured the battery of six 15-centimetre guns at Varengeville. They withdrew to the beach right on schedule. It was the high point of the day.

Allied actions on the left flank (at Berneval and Puys) were a complete disaster. A German convoy accidentally ran into the ships carrying No. 3 British Commando. As the German ships opened fire, the British landing craft were forced to take evasive action, and only seven of the original 23 actually made it to the Yellow Beach at Berneval.

The German defences were now on full alert and waiting. With all hope of surprise gone, the Allied soldiers who landed were soon pinned down and essentially out of the fight. The only good news at Berneval was that three officers and 17 men from No. 3 Commando managed to get close enough to the artillery position to bring it under intense rifle fire. For 90 minutes, at least one battery of German artillery was unable to fire even a single shot.

Near Puys on Blue Beach, the Royal Regiment of Canada and three Black Watch platoons landed late and were forced to come ashore as the sun was rising. As soon as they jumped out of their landing craft, the Canadians were pinned behind a seawall by heavy enemy fire. As more landing craft dropped men on the beach, the newly arrived soldiers had little option but to join the others sheltered by the wall. The attackers faced only 60 defenders but were unable to advance. The heavy German fire also prevented the soldiers from returning to the landing craft. The Germans killed 225 and took another 264 Canadians prisoner. Only 33 of the men from Blue Beach made it back to England.

On the right flank, the South Saskatchewan Regiment and the Queen's Own Cameron Highlanders landed at 4:52 AM, caught the enemy by surprise, and waded ashore before the Germans knew what was happening. However, the men hit Green Beach on the wrong side of the Scie River. With no other way to cross the river, the Canadians were forced to enter the town of Pourville to use the only available bridge.

By the time the Canadians reached the bridge, the Germans, anticipating their movements, had set up machine guns and anti-tank artillery to keep the Canadians from crossing. The Germans kept up a constant stream of fire, and soon many Canadians lay dead and wounded. Some of the Canadians, including the South Saskatchewan's commanding officer Lieutenant Colonel Charles Merritt, made it across, but they could not hold the bridge in the face of superior German defences.

Merritt and a small group of men set up a rearguard force to allow the Canadians to withdraw. Ultimately, 341 men made it back to the landing craft and England, but 141 died at the Pourville bridge. The rest, including Merritt, were taken prisoner.

The only success the South Saskatchewans achieved at Dieppe was a raid on the German radar station at Pourville. A small group of Saskatchewans were assigned to act as a bodyguard for RAF Flight Sergeant Jack Nissenthall, a radar expert. The men managed to get to the station and cut the telephone wires leading to it. With the wires down, the Germans were forced to communicate using radio; their transmissions were monitored by Allied intelligence. This provided the Allies with a detailed understanding of the radar defences along the French coast.

Nissenthall was grateful his part of the raid had worked. He knew that, because of his specialized knowledge, his bodyguard had been ordered to kill him if there was any chance he was about to be captured by the Germans. He and his bodyguard returned safely to England.

The main attack at Dieppe started with four destroyers bombarding German defensive positions. Soon five Hurricane squadrons were bombing any positions the naval barrage had missed, while laying down a smoke screen to protect the Essex Scottish Regiment (to the east on Red Beach) and the Royal Hamilton Light Infantry (to the west on White Beach). They landed at 5:20 AM and quickly made it to the protection of the seawall.

Both infantry units expected to be supported by tanks from the 14th Canadian Army Tank Regiment, but they were nowhere to be seen. Meanwhile, the landing craft had pulled back from the beach. Retreat was impossible, and staying at the seawall was suicide. The only choice was for the two units to attack. Whole platoons were cut down by the time the men reached the ruins of the shore-front casino. Some infantry actually made it into town, but without support they were unable to reach their objectives.

The Calgary Regiment did make it to the beach with some of its tanks, though too late to assist in the infantry assault. The regiment began with 58 tanks, but only 29 were able to off-load at the shoreline; the remainder were stuck on landing craft that could not reach the beach. Two tanks immediately sank. Of the 27 that made it to the seawall, only 15 managed to cross the beach to the boardwalk. They went no farther because of anti-tank obstacles and debris in the streets of Dieppe. The tanks retreated to the beach, where they were hit by anti-tank fire or became immobilized in the beach's loose shingle and pebbles. Turning their guns back on Dieppe, those tanks that were still functional provided cover for the retreating infantry. Unable to escape in time, all of the tank crews were either killed or captured.

For the reserve units waiting on the ships offshore, the battle at Dieppe was made all the more confusing by poor communications. The Fusiliers Mont-Royal, believing that the Essex had actually entered Dieppe and needed assistance, boarded their 26 landing barges at 7:00. Before they even hit the beach, they were targeted by the Germans and took heavy rifle, machine-gun and mortar fire. Many Fusiliers were killed while still in their landing craft. For those reaching the beach, it was the proverbial: "Out of the frying pan and into the fire." Of the 584 men of the Fusiliers Mont-Royal that headed for the beach at Dieppe, fewer that 125 returned to England.

Lieutenant Colonel Dollard Ménard of the Fusiliers Mont-Royal later wrote:

The second the boat scraped the beach, I jumped out and started to follow the sappers through the barbed wire. My immediate objective was a concrete pillbox on top of a 12-foot parapet about 100 yards up the beach. I think I had taken three steps when the first one hit me. You say a bullet or a piece of shrapnel hits you but the word isn't right. They slam you the way a sledge-hammer slams you. There's no sharp pain at first. It jars you so much you're not sure exactly where you've been hit—or what with.

For the men of A Commando, the other part of the reserve, their time proved equally futile. As their landing craft neared the shore, they came under deadly fire from the German positions. Lieutenant Colonel Joseph Phillips, their commanding officer, was killed in his landing craft while signalling a retreat. Fortunately his message got though, and all but one craft saw his signal and withdrew. For the few soldiers who did reach the shore, none made it more than a few metres from the landing craft before being pinned down.

By 9:00 AM it was becoming evident that Operation Jubilee was a complete and utter failure. Yet it was not until 10:50 that a general order was issued to abandon the attack and evacuate back to the ships. For the men on the beach, it was a welcome order but a hard one to follow. Even as the landing craft approached the beach and Allied aircraft tried to provide protection, the fighting continued unabated. By 12:20 the landing craft were no longer able to reach the beaches; 30 minutes later the destroyer

HMS *Calpe* made one last attempt before heading home. There was nothing more that could be done.

Of the 6033 men who headed for Dieppe that August morning in 1942, 1027 were killed (907 of them Canadians) and 2340 made prisoners of war. Of the 4963 Canadians who went to Dieppe, only 2210 made it back to England (almost half this number never landed on the beaches because they were held in reserve). The rest were taken prisoner. The total number of casualties was a staggering 3367. For the Germans, the losses were relatively light: 311 killed, wounded or missing in action.

Two Canadians won the Victoria Cross at Dieppe: the Reverend John Weir Foote padre to Royal Hamilton Light Infantry, and Lieutenant Colonel Charles Merritt of the South Saskatchewan Regiment.

It took weeks before the true story of Operation Jubilee came out in Canada. Canadians asked muted questions, but it was considered unpatriotic to ask too many. Yet the raid on Dieppe provided Allied planners with valuable lessons. It was clear that ship-to-shore communications failed at Dieppe, and a solution had to be found. It was also clear that the Germans were prepared for the raid, and if the Allies were going to successfully obtain a foothold in Europe, much more needed to be done to control information and intelligence. The lessons learned at Dieppe would be invaluable later in the war, but those lessons came at a steep price.

CHAPTER NINETEEN

Ortona, Italy
December 1943

TODAY, ITALY HAS THE REPUTATION FOR GREAT wine, romantic cities and warm weather. Tourists from around the world flock to the country to experience "La Dolce Vita." But in 1943, Italy meant something completely different to Canadian soldiers staring through their binoculars at the small port town of Ortona on the Adriatic Sea.

Ortona was of great importance to Allied war planners. If the Allies could capture the town with its deep-water port, they could shorten their supply lines and potentially the war. It would not be easy. The town, with a population of 10,000, was part of Hitler's Winter Line, a series of defensive lines south of Rome. The men of the German 1st Parachute Division under the command of General Richard Heidrich had been ordered to hold Ortona at all costs.

Only 450 metres wide, the town was a natural stronghold for its defenders. To the east, cliffs overlook the sea; on the west lies a deep ravine. The only street wide enough to allow tanks was the Corso Vittorio Emanuele. All the other streets were narrow and lined with stone buildings atop deep cellars—many of which interconnected.

Worse for the Allies, there were no natural avenues of attack. Coming into the town from the south meant that they had to stay on the Corso Vittorio Emanuele, which led through the town squares of the Piazza della Vittoria, the Piazza Municipale, and the Piazza San Tommaso. Each of the piazzas, and the Corso itself, left attackers vulnerable to being trapped in killing zones and raked by machine-gun fire. If the Allies stayed on the side streets and avoided the Corso and the piazzas, they would have to take the town block by block and, for the most part, without tank support.

Naturally the Germans were set up to make any assault on Ortona as difficult as possible. They blocked the main street, and reinforced and booby-trapped the town's stone houses and buildings. Stairways were rigged with machine guns designed to fire down on attackers, and explosives were attached to doorways and other building entrances. Enemy snipers, hunkered down in well-concealed hideouts, could control large areas of the town.

In addition to flamethrowers, mortars and anti-tank weapons, hand grenades were a favourite of the German paratroops. The many multi-storey buildings in Ortona allowed the defenders to rain grenades from overhanging windows on unwary attackers below. Many of the German soldiers had fought in Russia and brought a wealth of experience to the battle of Ortona, soon to dubbed "Little Stalingrad" by the Canadian infantrymen tasked with taking the town.

The British Eighth Army crossed the Sangro River on November 23 to begin the offensive against the

Gustav Line, the next set of defences in the Winter Line. Soon the Allies were through the Gustav Line and fighting toward the Moro River only six kilometres south of Ortona itself. Ordered to take Ortona, the British 78th Infantry Division crossed the Moro in early December, but the exhausted men were done. They were relieved by the New Zealand Division, but as the New Zealander's historian recorded, "the Germans were willing to sell ground, but only at a price the New Zealanders were not willing to pay." The Kiwis lost 1200 men.

The 1st Canadian Division was ordered to take Ortona. The Canadians, under the command of Major General Chris Vokes, were chosen because they were well rested and at full strength. Their first objective was to cross the Moro River, cover 11 kilometres of enemy territory and capture the junction of Coastal Highway 16 and the Ortona-Orsogna road—all within 72 hours. The 2nd Brigade of the Canadians would lead the assault with the 1st Brigade acting as a diversion. Vokes ordered the attack to commence on the night of December 5–6. Facing heavy resistance, the only Canadians left on the German side of the river at nightfall of the next day were elements of the Hastings and Prince Edward Regiment.

In an effort to assist Vokes, the 21st Indian Brigade was ordered to the Canadian's left flank. Supported by the Desert Air Force (including Royal Canadian Air Force Squadron 417), the Royal Canadian Regiment (RCR) pushed past the Hastings on December 8 and was soon clashing with newly arrived German para-troops. Simultaneously, the 48th Highlanders secured positions around San Leonardo, just south of Ortona, and prepared to push forward the following morning.

The next day the Germans launched multiple coun-terattacks. While supporting the Seaforth Highlanders of Canada, the Calgary Regiment lost 27 of its 51 tanks. In San Leonardo, tank battles raged at ranges of less than 100 metres. The Indian troops faced simi-lar resistance. Yet San Leonardo eventually fell to the Canadians, and the Germans retreated to the Ortona-Orsogna road. Here the enemy occupied a ridge overlooking a ravine known as the "the Gully." During the next eight days, the Canadians suffered 1000 causalities trying to dislodge the defenders. Losses were high because Allied artillery had difficulty locating enemy positions, partly due to the inaccurate Italian maps the Canadians were forced to use.

Matthew Halton, a CBC reporter at Ortona, described the scene.

> It wasn't hell. It was the courtyard of hell. It was a maelstrom of noise and hot, splitting steel…the rat-tling of machine guns never stops…wounded men refuse to leave, and the men don't want to be relieved after seven days and seven nights…the battlefield is still an appalling thing to see, in its mud, ruin, dead, and its blight and desolation.

The stalemate was finally broken when Casa Berardi, three kilometres to the southwest of Ortona, was captured after the Royal 22nd Regiment and a squadron of Ontario Regiment tanks outflanked the Germans. From his new base at Casa Berardi, Vokes directed attacks by the 48th Highlanders and the RCRs on German objectives. Within 24 hours the Canadians were in control of the Ortona road.

By December 20, the 2nd Canadian Infantry Brigade was on the edge of Ortona facing German soldiers who had been ordered "to fight for every house and tree." The next morning saw the Loyal Edmonton Regiment (the "Loyal Eddies") and the Seaforths, along with some armour, finally move into the rubble-strewn streets of Ortona itself. By noon they reached the first piazza, but there the fighting ground to a halt.

At first the Canadians could not understand how the Germans managed to quickly retake buildings and streets that had been won with such difficulty. They soon discovered that the Germans were using Ortona's underground tunnels to move men and supplies around at will. The paratroops even cut holes through the walls of connected buildings, which allowed the Germans to attack the Canadians from behind—from buildings the Canadians had just cleared.

On December 21 Major Jim Stone was leading a group of men who came under heavy fire from a German anti-tank gun. Charging the emplacement and disregarding enemy fire, Stone threw himself against the armour shield of the gun and then dropped a grenade on the other side. The entire gun crew was killed, the Canadian patrol was saved and Stone earned the Military Cross.

The next day Allied commanders decided to cut Ortona into sections and assign a battalion to clear each one. The Canadians recognized that in this urban battle, there was little command-and-control capability above the level of infantry sections. Yet, commanders had to know how the battle was proceeding in order to control the battlefield. It was discovered that the radios assigned to the troops did not work in the built-up areas of Ortona, so runners had to carry messages at set intervals back to headquarters.

The infantrymen soon learned that the less gear they carried in house-to-house fighting, the better. They left their packs at predetermined spots and picked them up after the battle. Carrying a lighter load, the men moved rapidly through the narrow streets and homes of Ortona. Of even greater importance, they quickly discovered that in house-to-house fighting, the ability to move silently was critical. The Canadians soon traded their army boots for rubber boots or even gym shoes, so they could move quietly and catch the enemy unawares.

As the German resistance intensified, the 1st Canadian Infantry Brigade tried to assist the men fighting in town by cutting off German supply routes to the northeast of Ortona. Canadian reinforcements entered Ortona on December 23 and 24. They replaced men exhausted by the efforts of fighting street to street and house to house.

The Canadians developed new techniques for fighting in Ortona. One was to concentrate the troops' efforts and, after capturing a building, clear it room by room. Orders were that clearing operations should start "from the top down," rather than "from the bottom up." According to a report on the Battle of Ortona written for the Canadian Army: "It was found that to clear a house from the bottom to the top was appallingly expensive...and for every German killed going up the stairs it cost us one of our own men."

German defences in every building were concentrated on the ground floor. The Canadians soon found that after capturing a building, the easiest way to attack an adjoining one was to either break through the roof or go through an upper floor. Using this technique (known as mouse-holing), the Canadians entered a building from above and threw grenades into each room or rained them down stairwells. As the men inside the building methodically cleared each room, troops outside covered all exits with heavy weapons, prepared to cut down any Germans attempting to escape.

On Christmas Eve 1943, the Canadians were fighting for every inch of Ortona, often house by house. The fighting turned brutal—and personal. When the Loyal Eddies and Seaforths were bogged down, or found a building too difficult to take through mouse-holing, they called in the Pioneer units, soldiers trained in the arts of both construction and demolition. Under the cover of fire from the infantry troops and tanks, the Pioneers approached the building and stacked explosives against the outer walls. After retreating to a safe vantage point, the Pioneers detonated the explosives, bringing the entire building down on top of the occupants. Tanks and infantry then moved in to mop up any survivors.

When it was too dangerous for even the Pioneers to approach a building, tanks and anti-tank guns were brought in to shell and collapse it. But the Germans also learned from the Canadians. In one incident the Germans used explosives to bring down a building on a large group of Canadian soldiers; only one escaped alive. In revenge, the Canadians exploded another building, killing two full platoons of German soldiers.

Slowly, slowly, the Canadians wore down the German defenders. The constant pressure forced German General Heidrich to commit his reserve troops, the 2nd Battalion of the 4th Parachute Regiment, to the battle.

Christmas Day showed no peace on earth, good-will toward man, in Ortona. In an effort to offer some normalcy for the men, Allied commanders provided a Christmas meal served at a church captured by the Canadians. Troops were rotated from the fighting to dinner and then back to the fighting. The Germans quickly figured out what was going on and placed snipers where they could observe the Canadians on their way to dinner. Losses on the Canadian side were soon so high that field commanders ordered their men to stay put. For many, Christmas dinner came from a mess tin.

As the fighting stretched into yet another day, the soldiers were not the only ones suffering. Many of the citizens of Ortona had stayed in their homes trying to wait out the horrible fighting that surrounded them. Christopher Buckley, a British correspondent who was with the Canadian troops, wrote:

> *In one half-darkened room there were five or six Canadian soldiers, there were old women and there were innumerable children. The children clambered over the Canadian soldiers and clutched them convulsively every time one of our anti-tank guns fired down the street.... Soon each of us had a squirming, terrified child in our arms.*

By now two-thirds of the town was in Canadian hands. Officers were reporting good advances throughout the town, even in the face of continued German resistance. Relief came when the 2nd Brigade's Third Battalion PPCLI, supported by tanks from 1st Canadian Armoured Brigade's Three Rivers Regiment, arrived to support the advance.

By December 27, everyone knew that the battle was over. Field Marshal Albert Kesselring, the German commander, told his troops that: "we do not want to defend Ortona decisively." Knowing he had no further reserves on which to draw, Kesselring watched as the Allied 1st Brigade slowly cut off his avenues of retreats. With 90 percent of Ortona controlled by the Canadians, Kesselring ordered a full retreat to begin the next day.

With the withdrawal of the German defenders, Ortona was completely in the hands of the Canadians by December 28, 1943. Taking Ortona cost the Canadians 275 casualties, including 104 dead— a number that represented nearly one-quarter of all Canadians killed during the Italian campaign.

But Ortona had only been the final act of what the Canadians came to know as "Bloody December." Total Canadian casualties for the month were 2400, which effectively removed the 1st Canadian Division from the fighting until it could be brought back up to strength. Major General George Brown described the effort at Ortona as one that drew the Canadians together as a cohesive fighting force. He spoke of the victory that built confidence between the men and officers, confidence "built on the rock of accomplishment."

There is no accurate record of just how many Germans died defending Ortona—estimates range between 100 and 200. However, looking back on the battle, historians believe that no more than 100 German paratroops were engaged in defending the town at any one time. Using hidden tunnels and barricades of rubble, the Germans were able to constantly rotate men in and out of the battle and hold back the larger Canadian attacking force. Nonetheless, Ortona was a victory for the individual soldiers, the Canadians who participated and the Allied war effort.

CHAPTER TWENTY

Juno Beach, D-Day
June 1944

THE RAID ON DIEPPE PROVED TO THE Canadians, and the Allies, that landing in France and forcing the German Army back from any beach would be no easy task. The Germans had established heavily fortified positions on the coast of France and were expecting an invasion at any time.

While the invasion would not take place until 1944, the Allied high command had been working since 1942 on Operation Overlord. The plan called for a combined Allied force, commanded by the Supreme Allied Commander, American General Dwight D. Eisenhower, to attack the Cherbourg-Caen area on the Normandy coast. While the French coast south of England had lighter defences and better beaches for an amphibious landing than the beaches at Pas de Calais (immediately across from Dover), the landing force had a greater distance to travel.

Choosing Normandy as the landing site gave the Allies another advantage. The flat sandy beaches and rolling waves of western England were exactly the same as those in Normandy and provided Allied soldiers with the perfect training ground to prepare for the coming invasion.

To conceal the ultimate landing spot, Eisenhower initiated Operation Fortitude. This involved the creation of a phoney army, massed on the coast near Dover, to convince the Germans that the attack was, in fact, intended for the Pas de Calais area. To make the ruse more effective, Allied intelligence agencies worked to develop inflatable tanks and trucks, and other dummy equipment, so that German spies (and reconnaissance planes) would indeed see an army. Operation Overlord's success depended on the element of surprise.

The Germans believed that if any invasion of France was to succeed, the Allies needed to capture a port where men and material could be landed. As a result, all French ports were generally heavily fortified, and as a result of Operation Fortitude, the Germans paid particular attention to the defences around Pas de Calais. To avoid this problem, Eisenhower and his officers came up with a plan that did not require attacking an existing port. Instead, artificial, portable "Mulberry" harbours were developed, which allowed for an attack anywhere along the French coast.

In preparation for the invasion, better landing craft for both men and tanks were designed and built. Based on the success of amphibious operations in North Africa and Sicily, the Allies perfected a number of weapons they needed to get safely to shore. These included the DUKW (an amphibious supply and personnel carrier that could travel directly from sea to shore), and Sherman tanks that could "swim" in the water and then travel on land.

The Dieppe raid also illustrated the need for better coordination between the air, land and sea elements of the attacking force. Since April 1942, Allied planners worked on improving the ship-to-shore communication systems needed to make the planned air and sea bombardment much more effective. Eisenhower was adamant that unlike Dieppe, the soldiers involved in the invasion of France would get all the protection they needed to help them reach their objectives.

Operation Overlord consisted of 39 divisions: 20 American, 14 British, 3 Canadian, 1 French, and 1 Polish. On the beaches of Normandy, five infantry divisions would attack along an 80-kilometre front: the British Second Army, including the First Canadian Army, on the left, and the First U.S. Army on the right. Three airborne divisions, including the 1st Canadian Parachute Battalion, would soften the defences in front of the amphibious landing.

Canada's designated landing area was code-named Juno Beach. Stretching for eight kilometres, the beach had been fortified by the Germans with concrete emplacements, pillboxes, barbed wire and mines. In the centre lay Courseulles-sur-Mer and the two smaller villages of Bernières-sur-Mere and St. Aubin-sur-Mer to the east. Defending the beach and ready to repulse the Canadians were three battalions of the German 716th Infantry Division, composed of

29 companies armed with 500 machine guns, 50 mortars and 90 pieces of various types of artillery.

Set for June 5, 1944, the plan for Juno Beach called for the 3rd Canadian Infantry Division and the 2nd Canadian Armoured Brigade to lead the way. Each brigade was comprised of three infantry battalions (regiments) and supported by an armoured regiment, two artillery field regiments, combat engineer companies and extra units such as Armoured Vehicles, Royal Engineers.

The tanks of the Fort Garry Horse supported the 8th Brigade (which consisted of the North Shore Regiment, Queen's Own Rifles of Canada and Le Régiment de la Chaudière), while the tanks of the 1st Hussars backed the 7th Brigade, which included the Royal Winnipeg Rifles, Regina Rifles and Canadian Scottish regiments. Supporting the tanks were the Royal Canadian Engineers who would ensure all obstacles were cleared. There was to be no repeat of tanks being blocked as they were at Dieppe. Once beachheads were established, the 9th Brigade, consisting of the Highland Light Infantry, Stormont Dundas and Glengarry Highlanders, and North Nova Scotia Highlanders regiments, supported by the Sherbrooke Fusiliers tanks, would land, move forward to secure the gains already made and advance inland as far as possible.

As D-Day approached, the Canadians were assigned specific landing sites. Juno was subdivided into two beaches—Mike to the west and Nan to the east—and each beach had specific sectors. On Nan Beach, the North Shore Regiment was on the left at St. Aubin (Nan Red), the Queen's Own Rifles were in the centre at Bernières (Nan White), and the Regina Rifles were on the right at Courseulles (Nan Green). On Mike Beach, the Royal Winnipeg Rifles were on the western edge of Courseulles (Mike Red and Mike Green), while a company of the Canadian Scottish secured Mike Green's right flank. The Le Régiment de la Chaudière was held in reserve.

Once the Canadian tanks and infantry established themselves on the beach, they were to move to their next objective and capture the three small seaside villages. By the end of the day, they hoped to be fully 16 kilometres inside German territory, just north-west of Caen. At this point the 9th Infantry Brigade and the Sherbrooke Fusiliers and their tanks would come up to assist. Altogether the Canadians committed 14,000 troops to taking Juno Beach, though only 3000 were in the first wave.

June 5, 1944, dawned stormy and overcast, and the invasion was called off. Reluctant to lose the element of surprise provided by the lack of a moon and favourable tides, Eisenhower postponed the attack until the next day. A reporter, who was beside Eisenhower when the invasion fleet set sail the next morning, later reported that there were tears in the general's eyes. Heading out into the stormy English Channel, where 109 Royal Canadian Navy (RCN) ships and 10,000 sailors joined the invasion fleet of

7000 ships, Canadian mine sweepers moved ahead of the invasion force to ensure the waters were safe.

During the early hours of June 6, paratroops landed behind German lines. Heavy storm winds buffeted them on the way down, and some landed kilometres from their comrades. Without tank or artillery support, 450 Canadian paratroops managed to regroup and, together with other Allied paratroops, capture a German headquarters, destroy a bridge and hold a number of crossroads until soldiers from the beaches eventually relieved them. For the Germans, the paratroops were a nightmare, because the defenders had to fight actions at the front and in the rear.

High above the battlefield, Canadian Lancaster bombers from the No. 6 Bomber Group dropped thousands of tonnes of bombs on German coastal defences, while Royal Canadian Air Force (RCAF) fighters beat back counterattacks by the German Luftwaffe. With air superiority established, the RCAF squadrons turned to assisting the troops on the beach by attacking the enemy on the ground.

Canadian destroyers opened fire on the beaches at 5:50 AM, destroying shore batteries that could have decimated the landing ships and their men as they approached. These same landing craft, having deposited the troops on the shore, were pressed into duty returning the wounded to England. But of the 306 landing craft used, 90 were destroyed before even reaching the beaches.

At Juno Beach the doors of the landing craft opened and the tanks of the 1st Hussars powered their way on shore and up the beach, providing vital cover and fire support for the Regina Rifles who followed close behind. For many of the Rifles, even an enemy beach was better than the sea-tossed landing craft they had just left.

They had little time to savour solid ground. The air attacks failed to destroy the German defensive positions in the Nan Green and Mike sectors of Juno Beach, so the 1st Hussars and the Regina Rifles had to quickly come up with a plan to destroy the heavily fortified German positions, or the Canadians risked being wiped out.

The tanks moved forward and fired directly on the German positions. The hope was that a lucky shot would go through the narrow firing slits and destroy the enemy guns inside. However, as the tanks were firing, they drew the defender's attention. This allowed the men of the Rifles to sneak up on the Germans and lob grenades into the pillboxes. Between attacks by the tanks and the infantry, the German guns were soon silenced, and the Canadians moved on to heavy house-to-house fighting in Courseulles-sur-Mer.

Most of the Royal Winnipeg Rifles and a company of the Canadian Scottish Regiment from Victoria did fairly well in their part of Mike sector. However, one company of the Rifles was not as lucky. During the approach to the beach, their landing craft came under intense fire while still some distance from shore. It was evident that the air and sea bombardment had not destroyed the German defences on the west side of Courseulles. Trying to reach the beach as quickly as possible, the Rifles jumped off the boats into the surf—some into chest-deep water—where German snipers and machine gunners killed many of them. Others drowned under the weight of their gear. According to the unit's war diary, "The bombardment having failed to kill a single German or silence one weapon these companies had to storm their positions 'cold' and did so without hesitation."

Pushing past the beach, the Canadians quickly cleared a path through the minefields and captured the coastal villages that were their objectives. However, the cost was high. Even with the support of the tanks from the 1st Hussars, the company lost 75 percent of its men.

Despite the best efforts of the RCN and the RCAF, many of the German shore defences survived the initial bombardments. Upon landing at Nan Beach, the North Shore Regiment and the Queen's Own Rifles discovered just how deadly the remaining German gunners could be. The North Shores took heavy casualties, and the Fort Garry Horse lost a large number of Sherman tanks, before the combination of armour and infantry overwhelmed the German positions. Other companies of both the North Shores and the Fort Garry Horse managed to capture Tailleville after six hours of very heavy fighting.

The Toronto-based Queen's Own Rifles also faced enemy gun emplacements that were only lightly damaged. To make matters worse, the tanks that were to soften the German defences ahead of the infantry's arrival were forced (by high waves) to land after the infantry and right in front of the German guns. They were easy targets and few made it onto the beach.

Those same high waves caused the Queen's Own landing craft to reach the beach a half hour late. In an operation as complex as Overlord, a landing 30 minutes ahead or behind schedule often meant the difference between life or death for the troops arriving onshore. As the Queen's Own Rifles landed, the only cover available was a seawall 180 metres away. Between them and the wall was an unbroken and unprotected beach. As the Torontonians raced for the wall, a German 88 mm anti-tank gun opened fire and decimated the lead company, killing two-thirds of the Canadians before the survivors could get off the beach.

Landing west of Bernières was A Company of the Queen's Own. For the soldiers in the landing craft, the battle became a very personal thing, because as the landing craft silently approached the beach 10 abreast, the assault fleet disappeared from view. As the landing craft ground up onto the beach and dropped their ramps, the Queen's Own came under immediate heavy machine-gun and mortar fire. Sergeant Major Charlie Martin described the landing in his book *Battle Diary:*

The men rose, starboard line turning right, port turn-
ing left. I said to Jack, across from me, and to every-
one: "Move! Fast! Don't stop for anything. Go! Go!
Go!" We raced down the ramp, Jack and I side by side,
the men closely following. We fanned out as fast as we
could, heading for that sea wall…. None of us really
grasped…just how thin on the ground we were. Each
of the ten boatloads had become an independent fight-
ing unit…. There were mines buried in the sand. On
the dead run you just chose the path that looked best.

On another part of Nan Beach, B Company of the
Queen's Own lost half its men before three riflemen,
armed with Sten guns and grenades, destroyed a German strongpoint—a feat of bravery that allowed the
others to finally get off the beach. The Queen's Own
paid the highest price by far for taking Juno Beach.

As the initial assault progressed, the reserve units
were quickly sent ashore. The Canadian Scottish
soon engaged the enemy, but the landing craft carrying Le Régiment de la Chaudière hit a mine. The
soldiers were forced to swim for shore—without
their gear. Yet, the Canadians were carrying the day.
By noon all units of the 3rd Canadian Division were
ashore, and the 9th Infantry Brigade was moving to
solidify the gains.

By the end of the day on June 6, only one Canadian unit had reached its final objective, but the
German defences were fully breached. Canadian
forces were as far as 12 kilometres inland and held
the villages of Anisy and Mathieu. While the

Canadians had been stopped five kilometres short of the Carpquet airport and were the same distance from Caen, Canadian tanks advanced far enough to temporarily capture the Caen-Bayeux road. While forced to retreat when supporting infantry failed to appear, it was a major victory—the tanks of the 1st Hussars had pushed farther inland than any other Allied troops.

As darkness fell, the Allies held an irregular front in France. In one day they had landed 155,000 troops in France, along with 6000 vehicles (including 900 tanks and 600 guns) and about 3600 tonnes of supplies. The Atlantic wall had been breached; Eisenhower's obsession with secrecy had been rewarded. The Allies were back in Europe, and the Germans had few forces available to drive the Allies back into the sea.

"The German dead were littered over the dunes, by the gun positions," Ross Munro, a Canadian journalist, reported. "By them, lay Canadians in bloodstained battledress, in the sand and in the grass, on the wire and by the concrete forts…. They had lived a few minutes of the victory they had made. That was all."

In taking Juno Beach, 340 Canadians were killed with another 574 wounded and 47 taken prisoner. The Canadians held the dubious distinction of having the heaviest ratio of losses to troops invading of the three invasion beaches assigned to Commonwealth forces.

CHAPTER TWENTY ONE

Battle of the Atlantic
1939–1945

WHEN WORLD WAR II STARTED IN SEPTEMBER 1939, so did Canada's longest running battle—the Battle of the Atlantic. It lasted for the duration of the war, and began when a German submarine sank the Montréal-bound steam liner SS *Athenia* with more than 1400 passengers and crew aboard on September 3, 1939. Four Canadians were among the 118 killed.

At the start of the Battle of the Atlantic in 1939, Canada's Navy consisted of a mere 13 ships (including six destroyers) and 3500 personnel. By the end of the war, Canada had the third-largest navy in the world, with 373 fighting ships and 110,000 officers and sailors, including 6500 women in the Women's Royal Canadian Naval Services.

When the Battle of the Atlantic began, the German Navy (the Kriegsmarine) was not able to directly attack the combined French and British navies. Instead, using submarines (U-boats) and pocket battleships, the Germans waged naval warfare on commercial shipping. Hitler planned to bring the Allies to their knees by choking off the vital supplies that Britain depended on for her very survival.

In 1939, Germany's U-boats (Unterseebooten) seemed to be the ultimate weapon. They could remain at sea hunting Allied shipping for as long as three months. Their arsenal included 21 torpedoes and a large number of land mines. They were truly vulnerable only when on the surface charging their batteries, but even then they could dive below the waves in less than 30 seconds and avoid the Allied ships and planes hunting them.

The Allies responded by organizing their commercial shipping into convoys: fleets of commercial ships protected by armed naval ships. The convoys filled two roles: the commercial ships could cross the Atlantic with some sense of security, and the convoys drew the U-boats toward them so the naval ships could hunt them down.

To the Royal Navy in 1939, the U-boat threat came as somewhat of a surprise. Because unrestricted submarine warfare had been ruled illegal by the Treaty of Versailles, British military planners had spent little effort (and even less money) preparing for the threat that was to come. Commanders assigned to the anti-submarine inshore patrol craft, which were equipped with hydrophones and armed with a small gun and depth charges, saw the duty as drudgery surpassed only by mine sweeping. Fast destroyers also carried depth charges, but because these ships were part of fleet operations, depth-charge training was kept to an absolute minimum.

Canada's deep-water port at Halifax became key to the Allied convoy effort. Ships from around the world gathered in Bedford Basin, organized into convoys and then headed into the Atlantic—just as they had in World War I.

A safe port was about all Canada could offer the Allied naval effort in the autumn of 1939, since Canada's "fleet" consisted of the destroyers HMCS *Fraser, Ottawa, Restigouche, Saguenay, St. Laurent* and *Skeena*. They were soon to be joined by the *Assiniboine*. These River-class destroyers were small but fast and armed to the teeth. On September 16, 1939, the first convoy steamed out of Halifax, with the *St. Laurent* and *Saguenay* helping to provide protective cover.

Canada was not only required to escort convoys but to protect her own shores as well. By 1940 Canadian shipyards were building 92 new warships: 64 corvettes armed with depth charges and 28 Bangor-class minesweepers. Canadian shipbuilding was being stretched to its maximum capacity.

Through the winter of 1939–1940, the Battle of the Atlantic settled into the seaborne equivalent of the Phoney War on land, as a harsh winter froze many of the U-boats in their Baltic ports. In addition, Operation Weserübung—Hitler's plans to attack Norway and Denmark in early 1940—called for support from most of the Kriegsmarine, leaving few ships available to attack Atlantic convoys.

When Norway fell to Germany in April 1940, followed by the Low Countries (Luxembourg,

Belgium and the Netherlands) and France in May and June, and with Italy's entry into the war in June, the balance of power in the Atlantic changed dramatically. With the French fleet now out of the war, Britain and her allies (including Canada) struggled to meet the maritime demands placed on them. Britain was now forced to extend her operations into the western Mediterranean, while a large number of destroyers were removed from convoy duty to assist in operations—first in Norway and then at Dunkirk. Finally, faced with the threat of an imminent invasion, the Royal Navy held many destroyers, including four of Canada's River-class destroyers, in reserve close to Britain to repel the expected German attack.

With Germany's campaign in Western Europe complete, the U-boats were released from duty in Norway and were soon back in the Atlantic sinking British merchantmen. The timing was unfortunate, because just as U-boat activity increased, the Allies faced a shortage of surface ships to fight them.

In May 1940, shortly after Winston Churchill became prime minister, he asked the Americans to arrange a "Lend-Lease" program for 50 destroyers the Americans had in their fleet but were not using. The Americans, not wanting to appear to be taking a direct hand in the war, agreed, but only in exchange for 99-year leases on bases in Newfoundland, Bermuda and the West Indies. For the Americans, who initially believed that Britain could not hold out against the Germans, the deal gave them bases where they could fight the Nazis before they reached American shores. Crewed by British and Canadian sailors, the destroyers ultimately made a difference, though valuable time was lost because the ships had to be rearmed and fitted with ASDIC, a basic form of sonar.

The autumn of 1940 saw rapid expansion of the Canadian Navy. As each of the 92 warships ordered earlier that year was launched, Canadian shipyards began construction of more warships as well as an increasing number of merchantmen. In addition, the Canadian Navy took possession of seven of the American destroyers lent to Britain. The American ships were used to protect Canada's very vulnerable coast, but it was soon clear that neither the American destroyers nor their newly trained Canadian crews were ready for the rigours of submarine warfare.

At the same time, the Germans increased their activities in the Atlantic. To improve the effectiveness of their submarines, Admiral Karl Dönitz, the U-boat Commander in Chief, ordered his commanders to cease operating independently and to organize themselves into attack groups that became known as wolf packs. Dönitz's plan called for the submarines to be stationed along Allied convoy routes. Since German code-breakers had managed to decipher the British Merchant Marine Code Book, the U-boats had advance notice of when and where the convoys might be found. When a convoy was spotted, the U-boat commander reported its location to headquarters. Headquarters then radioed the details to other submarines in the area. They converged on the convoy, surfaced under the cover of darkness, and attacked it. The results were devastating for the lightly defended convoys and their unarmed merchant ships.

The period between June and October 1940 became known to the U-boat crews as "Die Glückliche Zeit" (the Happy Time), when more than 270 Allied ships were sunk, thanks to wolf-pack tactics. During the winter of 1940–1941, the U-boats sank 227,000 tonnes of Allied shipping each month. Added to this total was the 330,000 tonnes of ships sunk by the Luftwaffe in early 1941 using land-based bombers such as the Focke-Wulf 200 and the Junkers 290. Supporting the U-boats were 32 Italian submarines that sank 109 ships in the Atlantic.

The Allies not only faced the wolf packs but also attacks by German surface ships on their convoys. By the summer of 1940, German raiders were constantly harassing the convoys, forcing the Allies to divert more and more resources to escort duty. Great battles between the Allied and German fleets dominated the headlines throughout 1940 and 1941. The German ship *Admiral Graf Spree* was sunk at the Battle of River Plate, while the British battleship HMS *Hood* sank, with only three survivors of a crew of 1418, during the Battle of the Denmark Strait. Finally, on May 27, 1941, an Allied force sank the German battleship *Bismarck*. This marked the end of the great naval surface battles and a return to concentrated submarine warfare.

Throughout the first half of 1941 the Allies tried to find new ways of countering the German threat. Even as more and more of the American Lease-Lend destroyers gradually entered service, the Canadian government started to build large numbers of Flower-class corvettes. These ships were cheap and quick to construct and, manned by Canadian crews, they rapidly formed the backbone of a quickly growing Canadian Navy.

Within a span of 10 days in March, Allied destroyers and corvettes sunk *U-47, U-100* and *U-99*. While the loss of three U-boats was not of particular significance to Dönitz, the loss of his three best U-boat captains was momentous. Dönitz felt it was time to change tactics, so he ordered his submarines to hunt farther west in order to hit the convoys before their escorts had joined up with them.

At first the U-boats were extremely successful in their new hunting grounds. Throughout April 1941, the U-boats again sunk large numbers of Allied ships. But the Allies countered. The escorts arrived early and started protecting the convoys at the very beginning of their journey. It was move and counter-move in the Battle of the Atlantic.

On May 9 the Allies scored an intelligence coup that helped change the course of the war. When the British destroyer HMS *Bulldog* captured *U-110*, an intact Enigma machine was found on board. The Enigma machine was used for the encryption and decryption of messages and was so complex that it had stymied Allied code breakers since its introduction. Now one was in the hands of Allied intelligence, and it was used to guide Allied activities in the Atlantic. Germany had inadvertently given up her communications secrets to the enemy.

May 1941 saw other changes for the ever-growing Canadian navy. The Allies asked the Canadians to take over responsibility for protecting the cargo ships as they moved past the coast of what was then the British colony of Newfoundland. (Newfoundland became a province of Canada in 1949.) These new duties required Canada to build a naval base in St. John's, Newfoundland, in order to service the warships that travelled from Halifax to Iceland and back.

The new Newfoundland Escort Force was commanded by the Royal Canadian Navy's Commodore Leonard W. Murray. On June 13 he took command of six Canadian destroyers and 17 corvettes, together with seven destroyers, three sloops and five corvettes from the Royal Navy.

These ships had a new secret weapon on board. Until 1941 the only electronic detection system available to Allied warships was the Allied Submarine Detection Investigation Committee (ASDIC), which could find submarines only when they were submerged. When HF/DF (High-Frequency Direction-Finding) equipment—Huff-Duff—was perfected, Allied warships could locate the wolf packs on the surface when they used radio transmissions to coordinate their attacks. For the first time in the war, the Allies gained the upper hand.

Various new technologies and strategies also helped defend the convoys against the submarine threat. New types of depth charges gave the destroyers a better chance of killing the U-boats underwater. Another innovation saw a few merchant ships fitted with a catapult that could launch a Hurricane fighter. When a German aircraft was spotted, the Hurricane was launched, drove off the attacker and then ditched in the ocean, while its pilot parachuted to safety and rescue by the convoy he was protecting.

Even though the Allies developed improved defensive tactics to protect the convoys, the U-boats still successfully harassed and destroyed Allied shipping. The Canadian Flower-class corvettes helped but were purely defensive; they were too slow to chase down the U-boats. By the autumn of 1941, the Germans had brought 585 U-boats into service, and the Allies were just not sinking enough of them.

Allied shipping losses remained high throughout the rest of the year. June 1941 saw the Allies lose more than 450,000 tonnes of shipping to the roving wolf packs. In addition to building ships, Canadian harbours and shipyards on the East Coast became the centres of a booming repair industry as literally thousands of damaged Allied ships limped in for repairs. The Royal Navy dockyard in Halifax operated 24 hours a day, training sailors and supplying the ships heading out on Atlantic convoy runs.

On December 7, 1941, Japan attacked the American fleet at Pearl Harbor. That single military operation in the Pacific Ocean dramatically changed the war in the Atlantic. The United States declared war not just on Japan but on her allies Germany and Italy as well. For Dönitz, it meant that he had to move valuable U-boats from European waters to the coast of America to engage American convoys that were now committed to carrying hundreds of thousands of tonnes of war materials to Europe.

Dönitz had only five long-range U-boats to use in Operation Drumbeat, his plan for attacking U.S. shipping. The German submarines took advantage of American inexperience in protecting convoys and scored impressive victories. Stationed off the American coast from January 3 to February 6, 1942, the five U-boats sank more than 135,000 tonnes of American ships.

Other submarines, refuelled at sea, began reaching the coast of North America. In just six months the new boats sank 397 ships, totalling more than 1.8 million tonnes of losses. For Canada, this new activity brought the submarine war very close to home. In January 1942 a number of Allied ships were sunk by a wolf pack of eight U-boats just off the coasts of Newfoundland and Nova Scotia. The attacks caused the Canadian Navy to reinforce its coastal patrols, which in turn forced some of the U-boats south into American waters. Yet, the U-boats never stopped hunting in the waters off Canada's East

Coast, and by war's end they sunk more than 70 Allied ships in Canadian waters.

By May the Americans had implemented a full convoy system based on the British model. However, fighting a war on two oceans meant the American Navy could not cover all the convoys all the time. U-boats continued harassing the American convoys throughout the Caribbean and the Gulf of Mexico. So Canada stepped in to assist the American convoys. Canadian ships from Newfoundland sailed south to New York and returned with the American convoys that would then join the larger Allied convoys heading for Britain. Eventually British warships arrived to reinforce the American convoys.

In Germany, Operation Drumbeat was seen to be so successful that Hitler fully endorsed Dönitz's plan to increase the scale of economic warfare on the Allies. Now Grand Admiral of the Fleet, Dönitz ordered the German shipyards to make building U-boats a priority. He also ordered his submarines to leave the American coast and return to attacking convoys between Canada and Britain. By now there were enough U-boats available that large wolf packs could simultaneously attack multiple convoys. Taking advantage of the fact that Allied aircraft could not cover the 500-kilometre-wide area between Iceland and Greenland (known as the "Atlantic Gap" or the "Black Pit"), German submarines sank 56 ships in that gap during October 1942.

Allied inventors continued to assist the convoys by devising new and better weapons. The Hedgehog, a contact mortar bomb, allowed the convoy escorts to increase their kill rate on U-boats from 7 percent to 25 percent. The Hedgehog only exploded if it actually hit a submarine, unlike conventional depth charges that simply exploded at a set depth. This meant that Allied underwater listening devices were not disturbed by depth-charge misses and could continue locating the U-boats. The Leigh Light, a powerful 22-million-candle searchlight, allowed Allied aircraft to light up U-boats at night while they were on the surface charging their batteries. Synchronized with the aircraft's forward-looking radar, the Leigh Light helped Allied pilots accurately target the surprised U-boats and gave the Germans less than five seconds to react before being attacked.

For the Canadians, the demands were unending. By mid-1942, fully half of the convoy escorts were provided by the ships of the Royal Canadian Navy (RCN) and the aircraft of the Royal Canadian Air Force (RCAF). In the air, the RCAF provided air cover for convoys for the maximum distance their aircraft allowed. In addition to the Atlantic convoys, the RCN was also protecting convoys to Russia on the Murmansk run and assisting with Allied invasions in North Africa, Sicily and Italy. To meet these demands, more and more ships poured out of Canadian shipyards, including 403 cargo ships of various tonnage, 281 escort ships, 206 minesweepers, 254 tugs and 3302 landing craft.

Canadian warships, many damaged from months of continuous, active service, were often called to Britain where they were repaired and upgraded. Even while the repairs were underway, the Canadian ships patrolled British waters and assisted with convoy protection between Britain and Gibraltar.

At the start of 1943, convoy duty remained extremely dangerous. In March, 82 ships were sunk in the Atlantic (120 ships worldwide); the Germans lost only 12 U-boats. For Britain it seemed that Dönitz might succeed in starving the island nation into submission. But the new technologies were finally starting to have a cumulative effect in the Battle of the Atlantic.

Perhaps the most important advance was the introduction of the long-range B-24 bomber. This American-built aircraft could reach the Black Pit southeast of Greenland and help provide the convoys with continuous air cover across the Atlantic. When Portugal opened its airfields in the Azores to assist with the anti-submarine effort, even more Allied aircraft could reach the Black Pit.

New ships were also making their presence felt. American-built escort carriers sailed with the convoys; their Grumman F4F Wildcats provided continuous air cover to counter German attacks. Inexpensive new destroyer escorts (also known as frigates), more seaworthy than the corvettes, became available in ever-growing numbers and were fast enough to take the battle to the U-boats.

Dönitz's warfare goal for the wolf packs was to destroy shipping faster than it could be produced by Allied shipyards. In March 1943, that goal had seemed attainable. In April, 39 Allied ships were sunk in the Atlantic, though at a cost of 15 U-boats. In May, 43 U-boats were lost while destroying only 34 Allied ships in the Atlantic. Because of these losses, the month became known as "Black May" in the German U-boat service, and Dönitz pulled his forces from the Atlantic. The Allied navies were now able to better protect the convoys and kill more U-boats than ever. By the summer of 1943, it was clear that Dönitz's goal could not be achieved, and the Battle of the Atlantic was all but over.

However, Germany still had some 200 U-boats available and more were being built. Desperate to continue harassing Allied shipping, Germany introduced a number of her own technological advances, but it was too little too late. When Dönitz ordered the U-boats back to the Atlantic in September 1943, they managed to sink eight Allied merchant ships and six warships but lost 39 submarines in the process. Even for Hitler the losses were unsustainable. By the end of 1943 the submarines, essentially defeated, returned to Germany.

Canada's navy continued to grow in size and responsibility. In early 1944, even as the Allies prepared for the invasion of Normandy, the RCN became the sole source of naval protection for the convoys crossing the North Atlantic. At the invasion of Normandy on June 6, 1944, more than

100 Canadian ships, including the River-class destroyers, were present to support the amphibious force.

With the U-boats out of the Atlantic, the Allies increased the number of convoys as the men and material needed to defeat Germany flowed generally unmolested. It was a turning point in the war. Yet Dönitz was still not ready to concede the battle. He had new, more powerful U-boats designed and put into production.

For Canada the new U-boats were particularly deadly. During the final 12 months of the war, 10 Canadian warships were sunk. Included in the list of ships lost were two destroyers, four corvettes, three minesweepers and a frigate. The final loss was the minesweeper HMCS *Esquimalt,* sunk near Halifax on April 16, 1945—just three weeks before the end of the war.

But these new boats came too late to assist the German cause. In late 1944 and early 1945, Allied land forces closed in on the U-boat bases in Germany. This forced the German Navy to scuttle more than 200 of its submarines and attempt to evacuate the rest to Norway. While on their way, the U-boats were located by Allied aircraft; 23 were sunk in the Baltic during the first week of May.

The last action in the Battle of the Atlantic happened on May 7 and 8, 1945. The Allied freighters *Sneland* and *Avondale Park,* and the minesweeper *NYMS 382,* were torpedoed by *U-320* just hours before Germany surrendered. *U-320* was located by an RAF Catalina

Flying Boat and sunk when the plane attacked the submarine. With the German surrender, 174 U-boats were turned over to the Allies.

Ultimately, the Battle of the Atlantic was a costly defeat for Germany and a costly victory for the Allies. The Germans lost 28,000 sailors and 783 submarines while trying to starve Britain into submission. On the other side, the Allies lost 30,248 merchant sailors, 3500 merchant ships and 175 warships (a total of 13.1 million tonnes) in their efforts to keep Britain and their other European allies supplied with vital war materials.

At its peak, the Canadian Navy was the third largest in the world, with 270 ships manned by more than 95,000 officers and men. Under their protection, more than 25,000 merchant ships safely crossed the Atlantic, carrying nearly 150 million tonnes of vital war material and supplies. The cost of this was high. While the RCN was credited with sinking 31 U-boats, it lost 16 warships to the submarines and another eight to accidents. In all, 2000 Canadian sailors died securing the supply routes from North America to Europe.

CHAPTER TWENTY TWO

The Merchant Marine
1939–1945

THE ROLE OF CANADA'S MERCHANT SEAMEN is a story lost in history. They did not have dashing uniforms or chests full of medals. They sailed on ships, some of which could barely make 10 knots, that carried food, coal and the many other mundane items required to win a war. Yet, at the end of World War II, Rear Admiral Leonard Murray, Commander in Chief, Canadian North Atlantic, said, "the Battle of the Atlantic was not won by any Navy or Air Force, it was won by the courage, fortitude and determination of the British and Allied Merchant Navy."

Britain declared war on Germany on September 3, 1939; Canada followed one week later. However, one week earlier, the Canadian government, reacting to intelligence reports that war was imminent in Europe, ordered all privately owned Canadian-flagged ships to be turned over to the Royal Canadian Navy (RCN). For the duration of the war, all shipping was under the direct control of the navy.

It was not a large fleet of merchantmen. In 1939, Canada had 38 small, ocean-going merchant ships that averaged 6000 tonnes each, crewed by a total of 1450 sailors. There was also the Canadian Great

Lakes Fleet, of which 133 ships were converted to ocean-going vessels during the course of the war. On shore, volunteers flocked to recruiting stations across the country as the 1st Canadian Infantry Division prepared to sail to England. Coastal defences were prepared and militia units increased training.

To Britain, her former colony (Canada) was vitally important. A single merchant ship of 10,000 tonnes could carry enough food and supplies to sustain 225,000 people for a week. Canada's small merchant navy was needed to carry clothing, fuel, steel, aluminum, lumber, aircraft, tanks, jeeps, trucks, guns and munitions across the Atlantic to Britain.

Canada did not have to wait long for the conflict to become very real. Immediately after Britain declared war, a German U-boat sank the steamship SS *Athenia*, bound for Montréal. Four Canadians were among the 118 passengers and crew killed in the attack.

It was soon clear to Allied planners that German submarines, the U-boats, were the greatest threat to the war effort. Hitler made it clear that his intent was to either starve Britain into submission or leave her so weak that she could not resist a German invasion. A critical component to Hitler's plan was to cut off the supplies flowing by ship to Britain from her Allies and the United States. He ordered the U-boats to sink as many Allied cargo vessels as possible.

With the declaration of war, Britain and Canada revived a World War I concept of moving large numbers of ships together across the Atlantic with armed escorts—the convoy. Convoys heading from Canada to Britain assembled in Halifax, picked up their armed escorts off the coast of Canada and sailed into the treacherous waters of the northern Atlantic. Eighteen ships in the convoy HX-1, guarded by the cruisers HM *Berwick* and HM *York,* and by the Canadian destroyers *St. Laurent* and *Saguenay,* left Halifax on September 16, 1939. They were the first to challenge the gauntlet of U-boats. The warships, and the Royal Canadian Air Force (RCAF) planes flying overhead, returned to Halifax once the convoy was safely away from the Canadian coast. Met by the Royal Navy off the coast of Ireland, Convoy HX-1 arrived safely in England.

The first convoys usually consisted of as many as 40 merchant vessels, arranged in 10 columns of four ships each. Headed by a flagship and protected on the flanks by warships, the merchantmen initially crossed the Atlantic in relative safety. Soon two convoys a week sailed from Halifax, and by the end of 1939, 410 ships in 14 convoys had crossed the Atlantic with only three ships lost to U-boats and German mines. Canada suffered her first merchant-ship loss on June 15, 1940, when the Canadian-flagged *Erik Boye* was torpedoed by *U-38* off Land's End, England.

The Allies were soon arming the merchantmen with deck guns in an attempt to give the ships some hope of driving off the U-boats, which preferred to attack while surfaced rather than submerged. The guns did provide some protection against the U-boats and Luftwaffe bombers, but German surface raiders easily out-gunned the Allied merchant ships and could strike with impunity.

For the men who sailed with the Merchant Navy, it was a difficult and hazardous crossing each and every time. The men came from across the world, often sailing in rickety ships, to face both enemy attacks and the treacherous weather of the North Atlantic. Rear Admiral Leonard Murray, Commander in Chief, Canadian North Atlantic wrote:

The toll in human life was mounting steadily.... Seamen whose vessels were hit hard had only a 50 per cent chance of survival. Death by explosion or fire or scalding steam, or by drowning in the malevolent grey waters as a ship was sucked under—all were horrific enough. Harshest of all, floundering men from fatally hit vessels frequently had to be left behind so as not to make sitting ducks of the ships still under way.... Stricken vessels limped back to port, their open wounds slicking the sea with oil.

In September 1940, the U-boats changed tactics from independent attacks to coordinated assaults by the infamous wolf packs. Stretched out across the Atlantic in search of their prey, the submarines attempted to locate a convoy. If successful, the U-boat surfaced and reported its location back to headquarters, which then dispatched all available submarines to the convoy's reported location. The U-boats coordinated their attacks and could destroy as many as 20 percent of a convoy's ships in a single attack. For the submariners, the summer and autumn of 1940 was known as "the Happy Time." For the Allies, the actions of these wolf packs threatened the very survival of Britain.

If the Allies had any hope of winning the Battle of the Atlantic, two things needed to happen: the navy had to find new ways to defeat the U-boats, and the Allied shipyards had to build merchant ships faster than the Germans could sink them. Both were very challenging tasks.

By this time, Britain's ship-building was near her capacity, so she turned to the United States and Canada for assistance. Due to the reduction of the Canadian Navy after World War I and her miniscule merchant navy, Canada had only four small ship-yards with a total of nine berths capable of handling ships of the required 10,000-tonne dead-weight-tonnage (dwt) category. The government in Ottawa agreed to assist, but it would take time—time the Allies did not have.

In June 1941, the U-boats destroyed almost 500,000 tonnes of Allied shipping. Three months later a convoy of 60 ships was attacked by a wolf pack of 14 U-boats off Cape Farewell, Greenland. Out of range of shore-based Allied aircraft, and with only four escort ships, the convoy was an easy target. During two days of sustained attacks, the U-boats sank 15 ships with 40,000 tonnes of cargo aboard and killed more than 160 merchant seamen.

Known as the "Battle of Cape Farewell," the action taught the Allies some difficult lessons. More escorts were required to guard the convoys, the men on the escort ships needed more training, the warships needed better technology and rescue ships had to sail with the convoys, since a man would die in the frigid Atlantic waters within minutes of abandoning ship.

As the Allies developed countermeasures for the North Atlantic, America entered the war after the bombing of Pearl Harbor on December 7, 1941. The Germans, sensing easier targets off the American coast and in the Caribbean, shifted their submarines south. From January to July 1942, the wolf packs sank some 400 ships and lost only seven U-boats in the process.

In response, Canadian and American ships began working together to protect the convoys as they moved from New York and Boston to Halifax. Escorts also accompanied oil tankers on route from the Caribbean. These duties taxed the Canadian Navy to its limit, just as the Germans struck very close to home in the Gulf of St. Lawrence.

On May 11, 1942, the *Nicoya,* a 5000-tonne freighter, was torpedoed 13 kilometres off the Gaspé Peninsula. Even as the *Nicoya*'s survivors were struggling ashore, the Dutch freighter *Leto* was hit and sunk in almost the same spot. Despite Allied efforts, the U-boats continued to ply the St. Lawrence. By October, 19 merchant ships and two Allied warships had been sunk. On October 14 the Battle of the St. Lawrence took an even deadlier turn when the ferry *Caribou* was sunk between Sydney, Nova Scotia,

and Port-aux-Basques, Newfoundland. News reports
stated:

> *The ferry had gone down so quickly that only one life-*
> *boat could be properly launched. A total of 237 people*
> *had sailed in Caribou: 73 civilians, 46 crew and 118*
> *Canadian and American military personnel. Only 101*
> *survived. Half of the military personnel and two thirds*
> *of the civilians, including at least five mothers and 10*
> *children, were lost. All but 15 of the crew died….*

The Canadian government, desperate to stop the
losses, closed the St. Lawrence to overseas shipping.
This action essentially shut down shipping from the
port of Montréal and reduced the amount of cargo
shipped from Canada by 25 percent. Winning the
battle of the St. Lawrence cost the Germans little, but
it had a huge effect on Allied efforts to keep Britain
in the war.

By the autumn of 1942, Germany had dramatically increased its production of U-boats, which
allowed wolf packs containing as many as 20 submarines to move against Allied convoys. While the
Canadian Navy also expanded, it still lacked the ships
required to effectively protect the convoys. The toll
on the merchant ships was staggering; 119 Allied
ships were sunk in November alone.

For the German submariners, the high point of the
Battle of the Atlantic came in March 1943, when
they sank 108 ships and 569,000 tonnes of war material. Yet, the Allies were making gains—they sank 16
U-boats during the same period and were beginning

to add new countermeasures that offered the convoys a better chance of survival.

As more and more escort ships were launched from Allied shipyards, they were equipped with improved radar units and their crews received better training. The construction of faster warships meant that the Allies could not only defend against the U-boats but also hunt them down and destroy them using new types of sonar and depth charges. A major breakthrough in the Battle of the Atlantic came when the British Navy captured a German Enigma encryption machine, a machine so complex that its code was considered unbreakable. With Enigma in hand, the Allies could decode U-boat radio traffic and anticipate attacks well before they came.

In Canada, the production of ships progressed at a rate that was described by the British Ministry of War Transport as "remarkable, astonishing and magnificent." During the course of the war Canada built 354 cargo ships of 10,000-tonne dwt, 43 cargo ships of 4700-tonne dwt, six cargo ships of 3600-tonne dwt, 281 escort ships (destroyers, corvettes and frigates), 206 minesweepers, 254 tugs and 3302 landing craft. By mid-1943, Canadian shipyards were delivering 3.5 merchant ships per week, or one vessel every two days.

Often more difficult than building ships was finding enough men to sail them. Ultimately 12,000 seamen were needed to crew Canada's new fleet. Boys as young as 15 and men as old as 70—ages that were a barrier to joining the navy, army or air force—could sign up with the Merchant Marine. Whatever their ages, the sailors of the Merchant Marine were a special breed. Frederick Watt wrote in his book *In All Respects Ready, The Merchant Navy and the Battle of the Atlantic, 1940–1945*:

> *A death in battle is not the worst way of going…. But there's no zest for combat when the sailor, trained to cope with hurricane or iceberg, with reef or traffic or fire, must endure his ship's crawling on imposed course in a drab huddle of strangers. All the while there is the suspense of waiting to see which vessel will be the next to burst into flame or a soaring cloud of debris, leaving a gap in the ranks of floating steel.*

By late 1943, it was clear that the Allies were winning the Battle of the Atlantic. The German Navy continued its efforts despite the change of momentum. In both the autumn of 1943 and again in 1944, the Germans used new models of U-boats in an attempt to once again bring back the "Happy Times." It was not to be, though in March 1945, the German Navy still had 463 U-boats prowling the seas. The U-boats torpedoed their last Allied merchant ship, the *Avondale Park*, on May 7, 1945.

Despite the Allies' ultimate victory, the cost to the Merchant Marine during the Battle of the Atlantic was immense. During the course of the war 25,343 merchant ships carrying 164,783,921 tonnes of cargo sailed from North America to Britain. Britain's Merchant Navy lost more than 1300 ships and 32,000 sailors.

Canada lost 72 ships and 1629 Canadians, including eight women. (About 90 percent of these losses were suffered between 1939 and the end of 1942.) Another 198 seamen were taken prisoner after their ships sank; eight died in captivity.

On May 10, 1945, the British Admiralty sent a message expressing its thanks, and that of the Royal Navy's, to the Merchant Navy:

...For more than five and a half years side by side with the Allied Merchant Navies in the face of continual and merciless attacks by the enemy you have maintained the ceaseless flow of sea traffic on which the life and strength of this country depend.... In this historic hour we think with special gratitude of the many merchant seamen who have fallen in the fight and whose service and sacrifice will always be a proud memory.

CHAPTER TWENTY THREE

Bomber Command
1941–1945

IF THERE IS AN ENDURING IMAGE OF World War II, it is of Bomber Command: large bombers, crewed by baby-face pilots, navigators and gunners, flying through the night skies and dropping bombs on German military targets in an effort to bring the war to an early end.

As early as 1935, Britain recognized that Nazi Germany was rearming itself and had placed a heavy emphasis on its air force—the Luftwaffe. On both sides of the English Channel, military planners believed that aviation technology had advanced so far that no country could survive sustained, high-altitude bombing.

Germany, focused on a total victory in Europe, planned to preemptively bomb Britain into submission before it could mount an effective defence. Germany's intent was clear to the war planners in London, and in response they established Bomber Command within the Royal Air Force (RAF). The objective was to do to Germany what Germany planned to do to Britain. Thus was born the concept of strategic bombing.

In 1940, the theory became a reality. That spring, Germany secured victories in the Low Countries and France. Turning his attention to the invasion of Britain, Adolf Hitler tasked the Luftwaffe with battering industrial, military and ultimately civilian targets across the Channel. Soon Dornier Do 17s, Junkers Ju 88s and Heinkel He 111 bombers filled the skies above England and rained down tonnes of high-explosive and incendiary bombs. British and Canadian pilots, in Spitfires and Hurricanes, flew endless missions during the Battle of Britain and shot down enough bombers to cause Hitler to first postpone (in mid-October) and then cancel his invasion plans.

With the German bombers subdued, Allied planners focused on bombing German industrial targets in the hope of forcing Germany's war industries to grind to a halt. Factories that produced war materials; oil refineries and storage facilities; and airfields, all became prime targets for the daylight bombing raids of the RAF.

Flying twin-engine Wellington and Hampden bombers, the RAF soon realized that daylight bombing raids only offered the Luftwaffe's fighter aircraft the same advantages the Hurricanes and Spitfires had in the Battle of Britain. The slow-moving bombers were easy targets for German fighter pilots, who shot them down almost at will. For Germany, the Allied bombing raids were considered little more than a nuisance.

In an effort to reduce both casualties and aircraft losses, the RAF ordered Bomber Command to fly nighttime raids on German cities. Initially this was not easy, as pilots and navigators had to navigate by the stars and "dead reckoning." For the Allies, the goal was to penetrate German territory, survive the ground fire from anti-aircraft artillery (AAA), successfully navigate to the target and accurately drop their payload of bombs on the correct target. To do this, long-range four-engine Halifax and Lancaster bombers were introduced, better electronic navigation equipment was installed and the concept of the Pathfinder squadrons was established.

The Pathfinders (usually flying the de Havilland Mosquito) were equipped with firebombs and flares. Their job was to lead the bombers to their targets, so the bomber crews could concentrate on accurately dropping their bombs rather than wasting time finding the target. On a May 15, 1940, raid on Essen, only three percent of the bombs hit Essen's factories. But led by Pathfinders during a July 25, 1943, Essen raid, the bombs from 705 aircraft hit their targets 96 percent of the time.

For Germany it was imperative to stop the Allied bombers before they reached their targets. German engineers developed ever-better warning systems, defensive aircraft and improved AAA. The constant pressure from Allied bombers ultimately forced the Germans to use 75 percent of their anti-tank weapons as anti-aircraft guns and commit more than 900,000 soldiers to man them. Factories were tasked with building aircraft and weapons to stop the unpredictable RAF bomber raids, instead of producing offensive armaments. Air warfare in World War II became a war as much about science and technology as it was about daring and flying skills.

Flying for Bomber Command was extremely hazardous. In addition to worrying about German anti-bomber defences, Allied crews had to be concerned about each other. They usually flew in a tight formation, in the dark and often in bad weather. Collisions in the air and crashes on takeoff and landing were constant dangers. Many crews did not make it home. As the flights of bombers returned home, ground spotters anxiously counted the number of airplanes as they touched down. The spotters then reported the losses to headquarters. If a squadron suffered more than five-percent casualties, they were reassigned to less hazardous duties. But it was not a permanent reprieve from battle. When the squadron was deemed ready, it was returned to the bombing runs over German-held territory.

As happened in the British army and navy, men from the Commonwealth countries such as Canada, Australia and New Zealand served alongside British bomber crews. Many flew in the RAF, but Canada soon had its own squadrons, crewed and serviced by Canadians, serving under the command of the RAF.

When war was declared, Canada committed what resources she had to two missions: air defence at home and the British Commonwealth Air Training

Plan. This plan saw thousands of Commonwealth recruits trained as aircrews and pilots, but it was a strain on Canadian resources. Even before the first all-Canadian squadron—the 242 Squadron— entered Europe to assist with the evacuation from Dunkirk, many Canadians had volunteered for service with the RAF and served in Coastal Command, Bomber Command and Fighter Command.

As the war progressed, the Royal Canadian Air Force (RCAF) committed to the idea of strategic bombing and assigned more men and planes to Bomber Command. The first Canadian bomber squadron to join the RAF was No. 405 Squadron in April 1941, which flew its first mission on June 12.

Less than a year later, the Canadians were able to commit 68 airplanes to raids over Germany, By the end of the war, as many as 200 RCAF heavy bombers flew in raids and dropped more than 800 tonnes of bombs at once. Ultimately, 15 Canadian bomber squadrons flew with the RAF, more than the number of Canadian squadrons assigned to Fighter Command or Coastal Command.

On January 1, 1943, Canada's RCAF was allowed to bring its eight existing squadrons together under an autonomous command known as the RCAF Bomber Group No. 6. Headquartered at Allerton Hall, and commanded by Air Rear Marshal G.E. Brookes, Group No. 6 ultimately controlled 11 air bases in Yorkshire by war's end. Group No. 6 soon joined multiple RAF raids on U-boat bases in Lorient and Saint-Nazaine in France. During the next 12 months, five more squadrons joined the Group, which flew a total of 7355 missions and dropped 12,360 tonnes of bombs in that time.

All did not always go well. While the Canadian officers quickly learned how to command and control units larger than squadron- or wing-level groups, the pilots and crews showed their inexperience. Loss ratios were higher than expected, maintenance problems plagued Canadian aircraft and moral problems were higher than in other groups. The Canadian officers demanded more training, and soon the performance of the Canadian groups had increased to the point where, over time, they were trusted enough by Allied command to be moved from the submarine bombing runs to the much more dangerous runs over industrial targets in Germany.

On March 12, 1943, all 11 RCAF squadrons were part of a massive raid on Essen, Germany. It was the second raid on the German city in a single month. The RAF attack group of 344 bombers was joined by 113 Canadian aircraft. As the planes lifted off, the night was clear and moonlit.

Once the Allied bombers crossed into German territory, heavy anti-aircraft fire rose to meet them. The AAA was directed by large numbers of spotlights that worked together in groups of 20 to 60 individual lights. A smokescreen, purposely set by the Germans to the north and northwest of Essen, obscured the city. But the Pathfinders led the bombers, including

89 remaining Canadian planes, to the target. (Mechanical problems and navigational issues prevented 24 Canadian bombers from making it to Essen.) The bombers dropped 450 tonnes of bombs on Essen during their 15 minutes over the city. Aircrews reported numerous fires on the ground that soon grew into a large single fire that engulfed Essen. A massive explosion, followed by two more even larger blasts, were reported. The fires could be seen from as far away as 225 kilometres.

Photos taken by reconnaissance flights the next day showed that the Krupps Works (a major industrial complex) had been severely damaged. The locomotive works, a key section of the Krupps Works, had 71,000 square metres in ruins with another 92,000 square metres of other vital buildings destroyed. In addition, some of the vital mines and collieries around Essen were damaged. At nearby Borbeck, a large zinc and sulphuric acid plant and three other factories were also apparently damaged beyond immediate repair. North of Essen, rail lines, sidings and rolling stock were damaged or destroyed, and the main line to Oberhausen was cut.

Later reconnaissance flights added to the tally. New electric furnaces at the Krupps Harbour Foundry Works were damaged and Krupps warehouses destroyed. At the Krupps Pattern Works the engineering and armament buildings lay in ruins. Aerial photos clearly showed that Germany's industrial capacity had been significantly hurt by the Allied attack. Intelligence sources on the ground reported that the Essen raid had stopped all activity at the Krupps Works for at least 10 days. In their most damaging raid on Germany to date, the planes of the RAF and RCAF also left 16,000 Krupps workers and 90,000 civilians homeless. The Essen raid was the very essence of strategic bombing.

Even as the bombers turned and headed for home, it was clear that the raid had been successful. But for the pilots and crews of the RAF, the celebration had to wait. As they limped home, the Canadians reported three planes missing, one each from No. 420, 424 and 425 Squadrons. In all, 23 bombers—five percent of the force—failed to return.

Of those that did make it back to England, many suffered severe damage. An aircraft from No. 405 squadron, piloted by Pilot Officer N.D. Daggett, was riddled with 200 separate holes from anti-aircraft fire, including seven in the fuel tanks. When the plane set down on the tarmac and rolled to a stop, the mechanics found that the "hydraulics, instruments, I.F.F. [Identification Friend of Foe] and the port outer engine were unserviceable and the rudder control column was almost severed," according to the Bomber Command, Secret Narrative, March 1943. Many aircraft landed with crewmembers dead or wounded. Some planes had hydraulic systems, electrical systems and radios shot away. Others were damaged in mid-air collisions and at least one landed with the rear gunner trapped in his turret. That same Secret Narrative detailed the heroics undertaken by the crew of a badly damaged bomber.

Many other incidents were related, but the outstanding one of the night was that of Wing Commander D.H. Burnside, D.F.C., and crew, of No. 427 Squadron. Their aircraft was hit by flak before reaching the target and the navigator, Pilot Officer R.J. Heather, was killed, while Flight Sergeant G.S. Keene, D.F.M., the wireless operator, had one foot shot off and cuts were inflicted on both his legs. The aileron control of the aircraft was affected and the windscreen de-icing glycol tank burst, drenching Pilot Officer R.J. Hayhurst, the bomb aimer, and filling the forward part of the bomber with suffocating fumes. Despite this, P/O Hayhurst directed the pilot to his target which was successfully bombed and a good photograph was obtained. Searchlights held the aircraft for a few minutes while over the target, but W/C Burnside skilfully evaded the defences and set course for home. All this time, F/S Keene, disregarding his wounds, laboured for over two hours to repair the damaged wireless apparatus. Owing to the damaged intercommunication system he could not speak to the other members of the crew, though they kept a close eye on him, and each time found him still conscious and working on his self-imposed task of directing manipulation of installations. He also offered assistance in navigating the aircraft and managed on two occasions to drag himself to the navigator's compartment to obtain essential information. In the meantime, the aircraft on its return trip encountered fighters, which Pilot Officer D.B. Ross, the air gunner, managed to beat off, at the same time issuing directions for evasive tactics that proved successful. Displaying fine airmanship, W/C Burnside flew his damaged aircraft safely back to base.

As the war went on, individual Canadian squadrons began to stand out. Based on its bomb-aiming accuracy, No. 405 squadron was assigned to No. 8 Group, Pathfinder, that specialized in target-indicator operations. (This involved dropping markers or target indicators on the designated "aiming point.") In May 1943, 331 Wing, including No. 402, 424 and 425 squadrons, was assigned to Operation Husky, the invasion of Sicily. Instead of the rain and fog of England, 331's Wellingtons were soon dealing with dust, sand and heat. Stationed in Tunisia, 331 Wing spent the next three months supporting Allied efforts in the Mediterranean. When other aircraft returned to England, the Canadian squadrons stayed on until October 1943 before returning to No. 6 Group. And on June 6, 1944, as Canadian troops stormed the beaches of Normandy, bombers from No. 6 Group dropped more than 715 tonnes of bombs on German gun emplacements and shore defences.

As the war drew to a close, the RCAF had 48 squadrons of all types flying over Western Europe, the Mediterranean and the Far East. For No. 6 Group, Victory in Europe Day (VE Day) on May 8, 1945, changed the focus of their flying from dropping bombs on Germany to bringing home Allied prisoners of war as part of Operation Exodus. And then their work was done; No. 6 Group was no more.

With the fighting finished in Europe, the Canadian government turned to the war in the Pacific, where the United States and Japan were still locked in grim battle. From No. 6 Group eight squadrons were assigned to Tiger Force, which was to perform bombing runs over Japan. Tiger Force began returning to Canada on May 31, 1945, in preparation for continuing on to the Far East. But the Canadians never saw Japan, as nuclear bombs dropped from American B-29's on Hiroshima and Nagasaki brought the war in the Pacific to an abrupt end. Within 12 months, all the crews remaining in England had returned home.

As they drifted back to their jobs in Canada, the RCAF bomber crews had a great deal to be proud of. No. 6 Group flew 40,822 missions against Germany's military might. The cost was high. In all, 814 aircrews did not make it home; 9919 Canadians died flying in Bomber Command. Of those who began flying with Bomber Command at the beginning of the war, only 10 percent survived. By D-Day (June 6, 1944), the odds of survival had improved—but only to 50/50. Three-quarters of the RCAF's 13,498 World War II casualties came from the bomber crews. According to Canadian pilot Murray Peden:

At times in the great offensives of 1943 and 1944 the short-term statistics foretold that less than 25 out of each 100 crews would survive their first tour of 30 operations. On a single night Bomber Command lost more aircrew than Fighter Command lost during the Battle of Britain. They fell prey to the hazards of icing,

lightning, storm and structural failure, and they per-
ished amidst the bursting shells of the flak batteries.
But by far the greater number died in desperately
unequal combat under the overwhelming firepower of
the tenacious German night fighter defenders.

After the war Sir Arthur Harris, Marshall of the Royal Air Force and the man responsible for sending the air crews into combat, wrote:

There are no words with which I can do justice to the
aircrews…. There is no parallel in warfare to such
courage and determination in the face of danger over
so prolonged a period…it was, moreover, a clear
and highly conscious courage, by which the risk was
taken with calm forethought…it was, furthermore, the
courage of the small hours, of men virtually alone, for
at his battle-station the airman is virtually alone. It
was the courage of men with long-drawn apprehen-
sions of daily "going over the top." Such devotion must
never be forgotten!

For Albert Speer, Hitler's armament minister, the Bomber Command's attacks were "the greatest battle that we lost."

Modern-era
Battles

CHAPTER TWENTY FOUR

Kap'yong, Korea
April 1951

FOR CANADIANS, THE END OF WAR IN 1945 held the prospect of peace and a return to normalcy. Toward the end of the 1940s, Canada was well into the process of downsizing her military, hoping to gain from what would later be known as the peace dividend. Indeed, Canada was focused on a long-lasting peace and was a founding member of the fledgling United Nations. Unfortunately, the peace didn't last.

On June 25, 1950, North Korea, supported by the Communist regime in China, invaded South Korea and drove deep into the Korean peninsula. The next day U.S. General Douglas MacArthur met with President Harry S. Truman and described the near-total collapse of the South Korean army. Recognizing that the loss of South Korea would leave the communists in a powerful position in East Asia, the American government decided they must be stopped.

The Americans asked the United Nations for a resolution pledging support to the South Koreans. At the time, the Soviets, who would have surely vetoed such a motion, were boycotting the UN and were not present when the motion came to the floor. The western-dominated General Assembly quickly supported the Security Council's decision to condemn North Korea and to "render every assistance" to the South Koreans.

When the Americans offered air and naval assistance, Lester B. Pearson, Canada's Secretary of State for External Affairs, publicly applauded the move and reinforced Canada's commitment to assist on the Korea Peninsula. However, Pearson was very clear that Canada would be assisting with a UN action, not an American one.

Pearson, knowing that Canada was well into its efforts to downsize its military, at first offered three destroyers and an air-transport squadron. The Americans felt it was not enough and, through the UN, pressured Canada for a larger commitment. On August 7 the Louis St. Laurent government gave in to overwhelming public support for Canada to do more in Korea and announced the formation of a Canadian Army Special Force (CASF) to support the UN.

As happened at the start of World War I, it seemed the Korean War might be over before Canadian troops actually arrived at the battlefield. As Canada was preparing the CASF, UN troops led by General MacArthur drove the North Korean forces back across the 38th parallel (the border between the two Koreas). To the world, equilibrium on the peninsula had been achieved. But MacArthur had other plans. He decided to destroy the North Korean forces and crossed the 38th parallel heading north.

Pearson was philosophically and politically opposed to committing Canadian troops to another overseas war. By the end of October, Pearson's greatest fears were realized when Chinese volunteers crossed the Yalu River in support of North Korea. Pearson and St. Laurent knew there was now no hope that the war would be over before the Canadians landed in Korea. In December 1950, the 2nd Battalion, Princess Patricia's Canadian Light Infantry (PPCLI) arrived in South Korea. By then the front line had again been established on the 38th parallel.

On April 22, 1951, before the balance of the CASF arrived in Korea, the Chinese Communist Forces began the "Fifth Phase Offensive" also known as the Spring Offensive, which involved three full armies—a total of 700,000 men. Four days earlier, the PPCLI had been moved out of the front lines to a rest area 25 kilometres to the south. Lieutenant Colonel James R. Stone and his men felt they would be safe so far behind the line. Then word came that the entire front was collapsing under pressure from the Chinese.

The PPCLI were ordered to immediately take up defensive positions on Hill 677. Located five kilometres north of the town of Kap'yong, Hill 677 is actually two kilometres of interlocking ridges that protect the entrance to the Kap'yong River Valley. The valley leads directly to Seoul, the capital of South Korea, 40 kilometres to the south. Hill 677 was 20 kilometres behind the line originally held by two American corps and the 6th Republic of Korea Division. But the Canadians soon learned that the

Americans had withdrawn, and the Koreans were falling back. Hill 677 had to be held at all costs to prevent Seoul from being overrun.

By the afternoon of April 23, the PPCLI were digging into the hard rocky ground of Hill 677. Stone tried to make the best of the difficult terrain by ordering Able, Baker and Charlie Companies to face the main east-west curve of the valley. Dog Company was on the left flank. Stone knew it was a risky position. He tried to cover the gaps between the companies with machine guns and mortars, and he ordered rock parapets to be built to protect the men in their shallow trenches. In front of the Canadians stretched booby-trapped approaches to their positions.

Despite being somewhat isolated, the Canadians were not alone. A New Zealand artillery regiment could provide artillery support, and a company of the U.S. 72nd Heavy Tank Battalion along with the 3rd Battalion Royal Australian Regiment (3RAR) were on the high ground five kilometres away. Captain Owen R. Browne, the commanding officer of Able Company, later recorded his impressions of April 23rd:

> ...suddenly, down the road through the subsidiary valley came hordes of men, running, walking, interspersed with military vehicles—totally disorganized mobs. They were elements of the 6th ROK Division...fleeing! Some killed themselves on the various booby traps we had laid...between 1530 hours and 1800 hours all of "A" Coy speeded up its defence preparations and

digging as it watched, helpless to intervene, while approximately 4000–5000 troops fled in disorganized panic across and through the forward edges of our positions. But we knew then that we were no longer 10–12 miles behind the line; we were the front line.

The Battle of Kap'yong began that night when the Chinese hit the Australian positions with infantry charges, machine-gun fire, mortars and artillery. At dawn the Chinese withdrew, only to attack again. The Australians, running low on ammunition and squeezed on all sides, were forced to pull back. While covering the retreat, four Australians from Baker Company of 3RAR distinguished themselves when they held off four separate waves of 200 attackers, killing 25 of the enemy and wounding many more.

By the afternoon of April 24, the Canadians were left alone to hold back the Chinese. The enemy was content to wait out the day, believing that they had the Canadians trapped on Hill 677. Before darkness fell, the men of Baker Company moved to cover the right flank, which was left vulnerable by the withdrawal of the Australians. They would take the brunt of the initial assault from the 118th Chinese Division.

At 10:00 PM the enemy attacked, led by soldiers blowing whistles and banging drums in an effort to frighten and confuse the Canadians. Soon, Chinese soldiers were close enough to throw grenades into the Canadians trenches. The PPCLI stood firm, but the sheer number of attackers forced Baker Company to slowly withdraw to more secure positions within the company's perimeter. Throughout the night Baker Company held off the enemy, often repelling them in brutal hand-to-hand combat.

At 1:00 AM on April 25, it was Dog Company's turn. Pressed on three sides by a large number of attackers the men were soon engaged in hand-to-hand fighting. Captain Wally Mills, fearing his company would be overrun, ordered the New Zealanders to drop artillery shells directly on Dog Company's position. As the shells poured in, the Chinese attackers gave ground. But when the artillery fire slackened, the Chinese attacked again, only to be driven off once more by the accurate fire of the New Zealanders. Through the night, 2300 artillery rounds fell on the Canadian's position.

Dawn on April 25 gave the Canadians a reprieve. The Chinese, badly mauled by the men of the PPCLI, withdrew to lick their wounds. However, no one on Hill 677 felt secure. They were still cut off from other UN troops, their supplies of ammunition were critically low and the enemy was still threatening.

At 10:30 AM four U.S. C-119 "flying boxcars" flew over the Canadian position and dropped food, ammunition and supplies. The airdrop itself posed a threat to the soldiers on the ground, since the pilots released their loads from a mere 60 metres up. While a few Canadians were almost hit by falling crates, none of the supplies ended up in enemy hands.

Fed and supplied, the Canadians prepared for another day of battle. It never came. The Chinese had had enough; there were no more attacks. The UN soon reopened ground routes to the front-line positions and even managed to push the Chinese back. Seoul was not threatened again for the duration of the war.

The men of 2nd Battalion PPCLI had distinguished themselves at Kap'yong. While suffering only 10 killed and 23 wounded, they held off more than 6000 attackers, killing 1000. It is true that the Chinese had outrun their supply lines by the time they reached Hill 677, which likely reduced their desire to continue the attack. But it was individual and unit bravery by the Canadians that carried the day.

Lieutenant Colonel Stone was awarded his second Distinguished Service Order; he won his first during the Battle of Ortona (in Italy) in 1943. The 2nd Battalion PPCLI was awarded a U.S. Presidential Unit Citation: "...in recognition of outstanding heroism and exceptionally meritorious conduct in the performance of outstanding services...." They are the only Canadian unit ever to win this award.

CHAPTER TWENTY FIVE

United Nations Emergency Force, Egypt
1956–1967

AFTER WORLD WAR II, THE IDEA OF CANADA as a country that sent soldiers to war was replaced by the concept of a country focused on peacekeeping. Canadians began to believe that Canada had entered a "kinder and gentler" era of warfare, because her troops were sent to danger zones wearing the blue helmets and uniforms of the United Nations rather than khaki-drab battle fatigues of a regular soldier. But peacekeeping can be a dangerous business.

In the 1950s the world was going through a significant change in geo-politics. Former colonial powers such as England and France were realizing that they could no longer afford to hold their colonies. Further, Cold War tensions between the East and the West meant that small regional issues could easily engulf the rest of the world.

Into this uncertain climate strode President Gamal Abdel Nasser of Egypt. After a series of deals made in an attempt to modernize his country, Nasser was ultimately rebuffed when the United States withdrew funding for the huge Aswan Dam project. In response, Nasser nationalized the Suez Canal in June 1956. The canal, owned by England and France,

connected Europe and Asia and provided a water-
way for transporting vital goods, including oil, from
the Persian Gulf. Nasser's action was a body blow to
the two European allies. Soon there was talk of
invading the Canal Zone and taking back the water-
way by force.

After striking a secret deal with the British and
French governments, Israel invaded Egypt on
October 29, 1956. Using the invasion as a pretext for
action in the Canal Zone, Britain and France advocated for a police action to protect the canal and its
vital economic links. Calling for a ceasefire, the two
countries warned that they would take military
action if Israel and Egypt did not immediately cease
hostilities near the canal. Naturally, Israel immediately accepted the prearranged terms, but Egypt
rejected them outright.

Egypt reached out to world leaders, lobbying hard
for support. Britain, still in a post-war mindset,
assumed that all of her former colonies would
support her. The weakness of this belief was revealed
on October 31 when Canada's Louis St. Laurent government refused to back the British call for aid.

By November 5, Britain, France and Israel all had
troops on the ground in Egypt and had effectively
neutralized the Egyptian forces. Knowing that ally-
ing himself with other Middle Eastern countries
would not strengthen his position, Nasser turned to
the Soviet Union for help. The Soviets quickly joined
the Egyptians and threatened to use nuclear weapons

against both France and England if they did not withdraw their troops from the Canal Zone and Egypt. Even the Americans demanded that Britain and France withdraw. The world teetered on the brink of nuclear war just a few years after the end of World War II.

In an effort to lower tensions, Lester B. Pearson, Canada's Secretary of State for External Affairs, visited Dag Hammarskjöld, the UN Secretary General, on November 2. During their discussions, Pearson suggested creating an international force that could insert itself, with the permission of all involved, between the belligerents. Pearson described the situation on the ground as "of special and, indeed, poignant urgency, a human urgency." Pearson and Prime Minister St. Laurent believed that with an honourable way out, Britain and France would leave Egypt without any country or the UN needing to resort to force.

With the threat of nuclear war hanging over their collective heads, the members of the United Nations acted with unusual speed. On November 4 the UN Secretary General, based on a recommendation from Canada, approached Canadian Major General E.L.M. (Tommy) Burns and informed him that a UN Force would be established to "secure the safety of the Canal, [and] police the withdrawal of the troops to the demarcation lines." Hammarskjöld's question to Burns: What would he need to get the job done? Burns replied:

I thought that the force should be so strong that it would be in no danger of being thrust aside, pushed out, or ignored, as the [UNMOs] had been in Palestine…. I thought such a force…would have to be about the size of a division, with a brigade of tanks, and attached reconnaissance and fighter aircraft units—the whole organized as an operational force capable of fighting. The initial form of the force should be [based] on [a] US independent regimental combat team. The force's units required the normal regimental weapons [plus] antitank artillery.

In the end the United Nations Emergency Force (UNEF) was not as strong as Burns desired. He later explained that, "only a few countries were eligible to participate in the force for political reasons, and many were unwilling." The UNEF ultimately consisted of six infantry battalion equivalents, and a reconnaissance and a support battalion, totalling about 6000 personnel—the equivalent of two light infantry brigades—from 10 countries. The UNEF lacked air support, had no tanks and received only a handful of armoured cars.

On November 7, 1956, Burns was officially given command of the UNEF with the mandate to secure the removal of Israeli, British and French troops from the Canal Zone (and the Gaza Strip), and to maintain the peace in the area. The next day Tommy Burns flew into Cairo on the first aircraft allowed into the airport since the British bombed the facility. His initial task was to meet with President Nasser to establish a working agreement that would allow the peacekeeping force to carry out its duties. One week later the Danes and Norwegians, the first contingent of peacekeepers, arrived. Burns immediately deployed them to Port Said to stabilize the area, given the loss of life and the physical damage caused by the French and British invasions.

But the Canadian contingent posed a problem. St. Laurent and Pearson had promised Canadian troops, and they had promised to get them quickly to Egypt. The nearest Canadians were the Queen's Own Rifles stationed in Germany. When they were proposed to Nasser, he refused their presence in his country, because the Canadian flag of the time had a British Union Jack in the corner! In addition, the Queen's Own had a decidedly British-sounding name, and their uniform was modelled after the British Army's.

Based on his administrative experience gained during and after World War II, Burns knew that more than enough combat troops had been committed to the UN force. What was really needed was administrative staff to look after communications, transport, supply and air reconnaissance. So Burns, Hammarskjöld and the Canadian Ambassador in Cairo managed to convince Nasser that the Canadians had an administrative role to play in the UNEF.

The first Canadian troops arrived in Egypt on November 24, 1956—not infantry but 300 logistics soldiers. By January 1957, Canadian troops represented more than one-sixth of the total personnel in the UNEF. Some 1000 Canadian solders (including headquarters personnel, a signals squadron, an infantry workshop, two transport platoons, and an Royal Canadian Air Force communications squadron), plus more than 100 tonnes of stores, 230 vehicles and four light aircraft, eventually joined Burns in Egypt.

In November and December 1956, United Nations forces concentrated on easing tension in the Canal Zone. The first step was to station UN troops between the Anglo/French troops and the Egyptians. Soon UN troops were responsible for maintaining law and order in the area and for guarding vital military and civilian sites.

As the French and English troops withdrew, the UN found itself taking on a larger and larger sphere of responsibilities. Soon Burns' force was involved in the administration of public utilities and services, providing food and other provisions to those in the Canal Zone. It even ran a prison for a short time. At the same time, UNEF troops cleared minefields and worked with the opposing forces to ensure that prisoner exchanges occurred without incident. As the Anglo/French withdrawal neared its end, UN troops doubled their vigilance in and around the Canal Zone to ensure there were no clashes between the Egyptians and the Israelis.

Burns quickly realized that peacekeeping would only work when it held the world's attention. Bringing his press liaisons together, he ordered that a newspaper be created to tell the story of the peace-keeping force. He even chose the title: *The Sand Dune.* Burns was right at home with the various writers who contributed both local and international stories; after all, he had been a writer in his university days. But *The Sand Dune* was a propaganda tool, and Burns made sure it was read at UN headquarters in New York. It received wide play and helped solidify the position of the UN force in Egypt.

Even as the British and French forces departed, the UNEF monitored Israel's withdrawal across the Sinai desert. The pullback was negotiated to occur in three stages: December 3, 1956; January 7 and 8, 1957; and January 15 to 22, 1957. The UNEF again inserted itself between combatants—this time Egyptian and Israeli forces. By the end of January, the Israeli Army had withdrawn from all but the Gaza Strip and the Sharm el-Sheikh region.

The Israelis continued to occupy Rafah, at the southern-most point of the Gaza Strip. They claimed they were awaiting assurances that the UNEF would administer Gaza when it moved in. General Burns journeyed to Rafah several times from his headquarters in the Canal Zone to discuss the arrangements for UN entry, without success. Even after the Israelis, under pressure from the United Nations and the United States, agreed to withdraw under the terms of the General Assembly resolution, Burns had to wait several days.

The delay was almost more than Burns could stand. Many described him as very quiet and orderly at the best of times; they had never seen him so frustrated and annoyed. His staff knew that he liked to be in control, but peacekeeping was not the same as waging a war. All he could do was wait until the Israelis were ready to move. Finally, Burns and his forces moved into Gaza on the night of March 6–7 and Sharm el Sheikh from March 8 to 12.

The UNEF then accepted temporary responsibility for control in the Gaza to ensure a peace existed between Egypt and Israel. To do this, the UN established an Armistice Demarcation Line (ADL) that stretched 59 kilometres between the two countries (from Eilat on the Gulf of Aqaba to Rafah on the Mediterranean Sea). It followed the international border as laid out in 1906, though Egypt retained control of the Gaza Strip. The line remained in place for more than 10 years. From 72 observation posts (OPs), each overlooking the other, UNEF troops watched the ADL. When night fell the sentries withdrew from the OPs. In their place, mobile patrols of five to seven men ranged along the ADL. The patrols were supported by a reserve detachment that could be rushed forward if needed. Day and night, a constant stream of communication flowed between the front lines and the reserves.

Minefields, observation posts and roving patrols were used to try to prevent infiltration from Gaza into Israel, Egypt cooperated with the UNEF by warning the residents of Gaza that they were not allowed within 50 metres of the ADL by day and 500 metres at night. Violators faced arrest and detention by the UN forces.

The UNEF worked under strict rules of engagement. They were allowed to use force only in self-defence. They could return fire if fired upon, but they tried to avoid any requirement to use force by working closely with both sides in the conflict.

Tommy Burns remained in command of the UNEF for three years. The force itself stayed in Egypt until mid-May 1967 when, in preparation for the coming Arab-Israeli war, the Egyptian Commander in Chief requested the "withdrawal of all UN troops which installed OPs along our borders." The UN commander on the ground refused and immediately informed the UN Secretary General of the demand. New York's response was to be, "firm in maintaining UNEF positions while being as understanding and as diplomatic as possible in your relations with local UAR [United Arab Republic] officials." The Egyptians ignored the UN and even occupied some of their observation posts. By May 18 the situation had deteriorated to the point where Egyptian troops refused to allow UN soldiers to enter the UN's observation posts.

On May 19, 1967, the Secretary General gave in and ordered UN troops to start an evacuation from Egypt. War between the Arab countries and Israel broke out on June 5, trapping some UNEF troops in Gaza. While all were gone by June 13, 15 UN troops were killed in the intervening days. In total, 32 Canadians died serving the UN in Egypt during the years of the United Nations Emergency Force.

CHAPTER TWENTY SIX

Medak Pocket, Yugoslavia
September 1993

AFTER 29 YEARS OF RELATIVELY STABLE AND quiet peacekeeping activities on Cyprus, Canadians had settled into a new reality. Canada was no longer a nation of warriors but a nation of peacekeepers. Few, including the politicians, were ready for the devastating and brutal war in the former Yugoslavia into which Canadian peacekeepers were thrust.

Since its inception in 1946, the Socialist Federal Republic of Yugoslavia had been held together by the strongman General Josip Tito. His death in 1980 was followed by a weakening of the communist central government. During the late 1980s, each of the six Yugoslav republics—Serbia, Slovenia, Croatia, Bosnia and Herzegovina, Macedonia, and Montenegro—fell under the influence of extreme nationalism that was driven by race and faith. In 1991 Slovenia, Croatia, and Bosnia and Herzegovina all declared independence.

These culturally diverse republics were soon fighting two separate civil wars with the combatants, mostly untrained civilians, supported by hired mercenaries. The conflict rapidly degenerated to civilians attacking civilians, assaults often based on past history and age-old grievances. The world soon heard of atrocities described as "ethnic cleansing" being undertaken across the republics.

By November 1991 the civil war in Croatia had ground to a stalemate, and both sides were ready for a ceasefire. In response, the United Nations established the United Nations Protection Force (UNPROFOR) and four United Nations Protected Areas (UNPA). Other contested areas not controlled by the UN became known as Pink Zones. Immediately adjacent to UNPA South was an area known as the Medak Pocket—a salient held by the Serbs. It was here that Canada engaged in its most vicious firefight since the Korean War.

Canadian support for the UNPROFOR consisted of an infantry battle group built around the 2nd Battalion Princess Patricia's Canadian Light Infantry (2 PPCLI). Commanded by Lieutenant Colonel James Calvin, the force, known as CANBAT 1, sent observers to Croatia to better understand the task ahead of it. These observers returned to Canada and delivered the news that the vicious fighting was nothing like the action in Cyprus, and it would require a complete rethink of peacekeeping. Calvin later testified that:

> ...peacekeeping had "evolved" in dangerous new ways since the 1970s and 1980s, and Canadian soldiers found themselves in a totally new environment. They were no longer interposing themselves between two parties who had agreed to a ceasefire. The situation

was far more "warlike," and called for determined
action and the ability to defend themselves and
innocent civilians.

Even before leaving Canada, Calvin insisted that
the 375 regular-force Patricias, 165 soldiers from
other regular-force units and 385 reservists deploy as
a fully mechanized unit consisting of M-113
Armoured Personnel Carriers (APCs),Tube-
launched, Optically-tracked, Wire-guided (TOW)
anti-tank missiles, an 8 mm mortar platoon, an
assault pioneer platoon and four rifle companies. The
United Nations argued that the force Canada
proposed was far too aggressive for peacekeeping
duties. Calvin would not back down.

When the Canadians arrived in Croatia in March
1993, they were deployed to UNPA West. By July,
French General Cot, the commander of UN forces,
saw an opportunity to force UN troops between the
two warring factions and drive them apart. The
Canadians were ordered to UNPA South, which
spread them over a 2500-square-kilometre area.

As the Serbs and Croats reinforced their positions,
the UN tried to negotiate with both sides. But while
continuing to talk, the Croats decided to drive the
Serbs out of the Medak Pocket in order to stop
the Serbs from shelling Croat positions from the
pocket. For the Canadians, their position suddenly
became much more dangerous.

Despite being reinforced by French troops, the
Canadians were ill-prepared to face a well-armed

and motivated Serb Army on one side and a similarly prepared Croat Army on the other. To make matters worse, the Serbs did not believe the motives of the UN peacekeepers, as they felt the UN was favouring the Croats and therefore could not be trusted. On the other hand, the Croats saw the Canadians establishing their positions within the Serb lines, right next to the Serbian Headquarters, and thought the Serbs were being favoured. The situation was explosive.

On September 9, 1993, Calvin received reports that the Croats had begun heavy artillery shelling all along the line separating the Croats and Serbs. Medak House, the main Canadian position, was caught in the crossfire. During the next 24 hours, 500 shells landed within 400 metres of the Canadians, completely cutting off the peacekeepers from both headquarters and help. There was little the Canadians in Medak House could do as the Rules of Engagement prevented them from firing on either side.

When the shelling stopped, Croat ground forces, supported by tanks, moved forward. The Croats made early gains as their Special Forces troops drove the Serbs ahead of them. However, on the afternoon of September 10, 800 Serb soldiers and 12 tanks arrived by train, with another 1000 troops arriving by truck, to bolster the Serb defensive positions.

Confined by the Rules of Engagement, Calvin could do little to help his troops, despite the fact that the Croats had captured 22 kilometres of Serb territory and driven 1300 people from their homes. As both sides tried to reassess their positions, a cease-fire was established that lasted until September 14.

As part of the ceasefire, it was agreed that the Croats would return to their September 9 positions, and the Serbs would remain where they were at the end of the day on September 11. This created a gap into which the Canadian and French UN forces could insert themselves. Calvin pulled together a battle plan in the few hours available to him. General Cot emphasized that if the UNPROFOR was to survive, it was vital that CANBAT 1 be successful, but he warned that it was doubtful the Croats had informed their soldiers that they were to withdraw. It was a no-win situation for the Canadians.

Calvin's plan called for a buffer force to be driven into the zone between the armies. A group of Canadians would investigate breaches, on both sides, of the Law of Armed Conflict. Calvin's plan was divided into four distinct phases. To separate the Croats and the Serbs, Calvin ordered C Company and 15 French Company to move forward and occupy the Serb front line. Once in place, C Company was to find and control an area where other units could move toward the Croat front lines. With C Company firmly in place, phase three called for D Company and 17 French Company to move through the Croat front lines, followed by CANBAT 1 Tactical Headquarters and the Reconnaissance Platoon. Once a new defensive line was established, the Croats were to be escorted to their new positions by Canadian troops.

If all went according to plan, the Serbs and Croats would be neatly separated and a new demilitarized zone created.

At 2:00 PM on September 15 the Canadian and French peacekeepers started to execute Calvin's plan. He later described the situation on the ground as:

Sometimes [the opposing lines] were 400 metres apart, sometimes 1,200 metres apart; it varied on the terrain. But you can appreciate that if each side had now taken the point of terrain that was the most tactically sound to defend, the terrain that was in between them was what we normally refer to as a killing zone, and that was the area into which we were moving the Canadians and the French.

As Lieutenant Tyrone Green and 9 Platoon moved forward, his white APCs immediately drew small-arms fire. Thinking that the Croats had not received information that the peacekeepers were moving into the area and had mistaken them for Serbs, he flew ever bigger UN flags, which just drew more fire. It was clear the Croats were deliberately targeting the UN forces. Recognizing that he would simply attract more fire if he stayed put, Green ordered the Canadians to press on.

Basically we walked one armoured vehicle out at a time—just walked out about ten feet, took fire, waited a couple seconds, walked it out a little bit farther— and eventually just showed to the Croatians that we

*weren't leaving—we were eventually going to get out
in front of the Serbs and establish our positions.*

With his men out of their APCs and dispersed among the trees, Green ordered warning shots fired toward the Croat lines. The Patricias opened fire, finally able to respond to the Croat aggression. When a Croat tank threatened the Canadians, Green ordered a TOW carrier forward and the tank withdrew. Soon the Canadians had crawled forward to the Croat lines. An eerie silence fell over the battlefield.

Captain David McKillop and 8 Platoon also hoped that the UN flags on his radio antennas would help clear the way forward. He soon found himself having to force his way through a roadblock of Serb soldiers. As he manoeuvred into position, he ordered the men to dig in. With the Canadians caught between the Serbs and the Croats, the situation quickly deteriorated.

By 3:00 PM, 8 Platoon was under enemy fire. The battle began with a single sniper firing on the Canadians. When the shooting intensified between the Serbs and Croat forces, the Canadians fired warning shots from a .50 calibre machine gun. Instantly, the Canadians were engaged in a full-blown firefight that lasted, unabated, for 15 hours.

To try to relieve the pressure on the Canadians, McKillop argued with the Serb commanders on the ground to not bring up heavier weapons, which would only antagonize the Croats and rain down more fire on the Canadians. Even worse, McKillop had trouble making UN Headquarters understand that the Croats were deliberately targeting the UN forces. McKillop was astonished when he was ordered to "talk to the Serbs and get them to stop antagonizing the Croats."

It quickly became clear that the UN thought they were simply caught in a crossfire. But at 9:00 and then again at 10:00 PM, the Canadians were fully engaged in firefights with the Croats. The United Nations Military Observers still could not bring themselves to believe that 8 Platoon was involved in anything more than a misunderstanding. Exasperated, McKillop invited the observers to come to the Medak Pocket to see for themselves. The last firefight for 8 Platoon occurred at 6:00 AM on September 16.

Even as the firing continued, Calvin was negotiating with both sides so that phase two of his plan could be implemented. The Croats finally agreed to a ceasefire but insisted that phase three had to wait until noon the next day, claiming that they could not get word of the ceasefire to their troops any faster.

As dawn broke on September 16, the Canadians understood why the Croats wanted to keep UN troops out of the Medak Pocket until noon. A full-scale ethnic cleansing was being committed by the Croats. The Canadians could do nothing but watch and wait for the noon deadline to expire. Under the UN mandate, the Canadians were not allowed to attack the Croats head on, even if they had the weapons and troops to do so—which they did not.

At exactly noon the Canadians pressed forward in their M-113 carriers but were immediately confronted by a Croat roadblock consisting of a T-72 tank, two anti-tank guns and a line of Sagger anti-tank guided missiles. A company of infantry were dug in and protected by landmines. For an hour the UN officers argued with the Croats, demanding the access that had been promised. When Calvin arrived on the scene, he quickly realized the Croats were stalling to allow their Special Police units time to clean up the evidence of the ethnic cleansing.

More evidence of the new face of peacekeeping was revealed when Calvin, in frustration, held an impromptu media briefing for 20 foreign journalists who were waiting for the impasse to end. In an unusual role for a battlefield commander, Calvin described in detail the ethnic cleansing that was taking place and how the Croats were barring passage of the UN peacekeepers. He could not have been more blunt. "At some stage you've got to cut the bullshit and get on with the job. And all I've heard right now from the Croatian people at my level is a bunch of half-baked excuses aimed at delaying us from getting on with the operation...." The Croats gave in.

As D Company entered the Medak Pocket, evidence of ethnic cleansing was all around. Homes were burned, shell casings littered the ground and 29 corpses were found. Rubber gloves were strewn everywhere, indicating that other bodies had been moved. Hundreds of Serbs were missing, never to be found. Even farm animals had been shot. For the

Canadians, it was as though all of the Medak Pocket had died. Evidence of the ethnic cleansing, collected by the PPCLI soldiers, was later used in war crimes trials against the Croat leaders.

The Battle of Medak Pocket came at a politically inconvenient time for the Canadian government. It was busy dealing with the "scandals" of Somalia and Rwanda, and certainly did not want Canadians hearing about a firefight during which Canadian peacekeepers killed as many as 27 Croats. The government of the day quickly buried the story.

It was not until December 1, 2002, that the officers and men of CANBAT 1 were recognized for their dedication and heroism with a Commander in Chief Commendation Ceremony. The entire unit was praised for its actions and numerous individual soldiers received a variety of medals—late but nonetheless very well deserved.

CHAPTER TWENTY SEVEN

Kosovo Air Campaign
March to May 1999

THE FORMER YUGOSLAVIA CAUSED THE United Nations, and Canadians at all levels, to question the role of peace-keeping. In 1993 in the Medak Pocket, the Canadian Army found its role stretched almost to the breaking point. Five years later, and for the first time since World War II, Canada was involved in an air war. This new role surprised just about everyone, including the pilots and support crews assigned to the Kosovo air campaign.

Since World War I, combat aircraft have been seen as a natural way to obtain an advantage over the enemy. Aircraft provide speed and flexibility of attack without coming in direct contact with the enemy, something unavailable to an army. It was no different for the UN and North Atlantic Treaty Organization (NATO) in Bosnia and Herzegovina, as an attempt was made to bring peace and stability to the country. This took place despite the fact that in the various regions of the former Yugoslavia, there was no peace to keep—at least not in the UN's traditional sense.

For the UN, air power was a double-edged sword. The use of aircraft could certainly pressure the various warring factions to act in accordance with UN wishes and orders. On the other hand, air attacks might endanger UN ground troops when those subjected to aerial bombardment lashed out in revenge. Many countries argued against using air power but others, including the United States, advocated combat aircraft.

Without a standing air force of its own, the UN relied on NATO to provide aircraft that could operate in a combat environment. By February 1994, NATO planes were flying regular missions to ensure that weapons were not entering UN-mandated exclusion zones, and by August 1995, NATO's role had been expanded to maintain no-fly zones. NATO aircraft were soon used for multiple missions, and some of the results were positive. They attacked specific ground targets (including Bosnian Serb integrated air-defence systems), caused the Bosnian Serbs to not attack Sarajevo and influenced the decision of the Bosnian Serbs to sign a ceasefire agreement.

As the war spread, many political leaders felt that the air war could be expanded to tackle other issues and situations, including the ethnic cleansing taking place in Kosovo. In response to a 1997 request from the UN and NATO, Canada sent six CF-18 Hornets from 4 Wing, 416 Tactical Fighter Squadron (stationed in Cold Lake, Alberta) to Aviano, Italy, located at the northern tip of the Adriatic Sea. Canada committed the planes and their crews for only three months, but the experience gained during the mission was invaluable.

Faced with a rapidly deteriorating situation in the Balkans, NATO asked Canada, in June 1998, to again supply aircraft and crews. This time six Hornets from 3 Wing in Bagotville, Québec, were sent. In the face of threats from Serbian President Slobodan Milosevic, NATO and the Canadian aircrews prepared for what appeared to be inevitable conflict. Finally in March 1999, Milosevic's ethnic-cleansing campaign against Kosovo Albanians compelled action, and NATO forces began Operation Allied Force, an air campaign designed to stop Milosevic. The objectives of the campaign were summed up by a NATO spokesperson as: "Serbs out, peacekeepers in, refugees back."

As the Serbian ethnic-cleansing campaign continued, tens of thousands of Kosovo Albanians fled their homes and farms for the relative safety of neighbouring Macedonia and Albania. Less than a month into the air war, the UN reported that 850,000 people had fled Kosovo. UN planners hoped that the focused objectives of the air campaign—destroying Yugoslav air defences and high-value targets—would take just a few days and a limited number of sorties. No one predicted what was to come.

For all their preparations, the Canadians faced two large challenges in supporting the air effort. First, the Bagotville crews were scheduled for rotation home just as hostilities broke out. Second, in anticipation of aggression from the Serbs, the Canadian government had agreed to double the number of aircraft in the theatre. This caused logistics nightmares for the forces already in Aviano.

The Allies were also having trouble coordinating planes and crews from so many different countries. Colonel Dwight Davies, Commander, Task Force Aviano, recalled that USAF Lieutenant General Short, the Joint Force Air Component Commander,

> ...assembled all the senior national representatives and requested that we all tell our nations not to send or offer any more day, Visual Flight Rules, air defence fighters. He needed precision bombers, and particularly wanted multi-role aircraft that could be employed where and when needed. He then singled out the CF-18s (with their day/night PGM capability) from Canada as the exact capability for which he was looking.

The Canadians found that things had changed dramatically since the bombing over Germany in World War II. For instance, everything now took place in the full glare of a prying, and often hostile, world media. Any actions that occurred in the former Yugoslavia were reviewed over and over again, often on the six o'clock news. Canadian pilots went to extremes to avoid any collateral damage (civilian injuries or deaths) and the resulting negative publicity.

Whenever the Canadians were assigned a target, a Canadian Forces legal officer reviewed the mission. If the officer felt uncomfortable with the legitimacy of the order, the Canadian Task Force Commander had the authority to refuse the mission. Once in the air, pilots were told that they had full authority to break off their attack and return home if they felt any hesitation at all regarding the target.

Complicating the activities in the air even further was the fact that all 19-member states of the NATO coalition had to agree to each target that was chosen.

The Canadian pilots faced a steep learning curve. As the first NATO attack group, including four Canadian CF-18s from Task Force Aviano, entered Serbian air space on March 24, 1999, they experienced everything modern air combat had to offer. This was no longer an exercise over the wilds of Cold Lake, Alberta. They faced a real enemy with real air-defence weapons, including anti-aircraft artillery, SA-6 surface-to-air missiles and MIG-29 Fulcrum fighters—all of which were deployed against NATO during the campaign. As a result, NATO threw everything it had against the Serbs. Available at any time were Electronic Warfare, Suppression of Enemy Air Defences and fighter escort aircraft, communications jammers, Airborne Command Control and Communications, air-to-air refuelling tankers, and Airborne Warning and Control aircraft.

Ultimately the Canadians employed 16 CF-18s in Aviano. The versatile Hornets gave NATO planners the opportunity to use the Canadians in one of two roles: as a bomber using Precision Guided Munitions (PGMs) or as an air-to-air fighter. The Canadians never left the base without air-to-air munitions on board, and ended up flying 18 percent of their missions as fighters. However, it was in the bomber role that the Canadians excelled. During the 78-day air campaign, the Canadians flew 678 combat sorties and spent more than 2600 hours in the air. The

CF-18s delivered 532 bombs totalling almost 225,000 kilograms of high explosives. Overall the Canadians found their targets 70 percent of the time—equal to any other air force flying during the campaign.

The UN was surprised at Milosevic's ability to resist the air campaign. When it became clear that attacking purely military targets was not having the desired effect, the UN launched strikes against a variety of other resources. NATO planes hit ground troops, bridges, factories, power stations, telecommunications facilities and even political targets such as the Serbian state television broadcasting tower. This increased range of targets meant that all NATO aircraft were spending more and more time in the air. The Canadian aircrews were always either flying a mission or preparing for their next one. At the peak of the air campaign, Task Force Aviano flew 12 combat sorties a day with 12 operational aircraft and 24 pilots prepared to fly. When a Hornet returned from a mission it was immediately refuelled, rearmed and, with a new pilot in the cockpit, launched again toward Kosovo.

Such an increase in operational tempo meant that problems and mistakes were bound to happen. Weather caused many missions to be scrubbed, while others were cancelled due to operational issues. Of greater concern was the possibility of a bombing error as the number of ground targets increased. While three major accidental-bombing incidents occurred that raised questions about the air war, the Canadians were not involved (perhaps because of their precise pre-flight planning).

By April 1999, it was clear that the air campaign alone would not bring the conflict to a successful end. Many of the participating NATO countries were reluctantly concluding that only an actual invasion of Kosovo would bring the war to an end. American President Bill Clinton opposed a ground invasion, preferring instead to fund resistance fighters in the region with the goal of destabilizing the government.

Russian and Finnish negotiators began meeting with Milosevic to press him to agree to a UN presence in Kosovo. Reports started to filter in to Milosevic that NATO Special Forces were already in the county scouting weaknesses in the Serb defences. This may or may not have been true, but Norwegian and British Special Forces certainly were on the borders of Kosovo and Macedonia. When the Russian negotiators made it clear that, despite their opposition to NATO, they would not come to Milosevic's aid in case of a NATO attack, his resistance collapsed and he allowed UN troops into the country. The Special Forces on the Macedonia border were the first NATO troops to move into Kosovo.

The NATO air war officially came to an end on June 11, 1999. It lasted much longer than anyone had anticipated and involved more than 1000 NATO aircraft flying 38,000 combat missions. While Canadians represented only two percent of the combat aircraft flying over the former Yugoslavia, they took part in 10 percent of the Battlefield Air Interdiction (BAI) missions, which included Combat Air Patrols and Close Air Support. These are the most difficult and dangerous missions in any air campaign, and 82 percent of Canadian combat flights were BAI missions—the highest percentage of these flights during the campaign by any country. No one could accuse the Canadians of slacking off! All NATO members participated in the war—even Greece, despite their initial opposition to the war.

Had NATO followed its own doctrine of delivering decisive air power, the campaign probably would have been over much sooner. (Modern aircraft can dispense accurate and devastating destruction on an enemy—if the pilots are allowed to deliver that power without interference.) However, the ever-present world media meant that decisions were often made not for military reasons but political ones. NATO discovered that warfare was no longer just about soldier fighting soldier or airman against airman, but about political correctness.

While Operation Allied Force did not achieve either its political or military goals, at least the Canadians could claim a success. All Canadian pilots and crews returned home safely; nobody died and any injuries were minor.

CHAPTER TWENTY EIGHT

Operation Medusa, Afghanistan
September 2006

FOR EACH GENERATION OF CANADIAN SOLDIERS, one battle defines the horror of war and the height of valour. During World War I, it was the mud and cold of Passchendaele; in World War II, it was the rocky beaches of Dieppe. For the Canadian soldiers of the 21st century, it is Operation Medusa in the heat and sand of Afghanistan.

On September 9, 2001, members of the terror group Al Qaeda flew two jet airliners into the World Trade Center in New York City and another into the Pentagon in Washington, DC. Altogether more than 3000 people died in the attacks.

It was quickly determined that the terrorists had received training and sanctuary from the Taliban government of Afghanistan. Within days of the attack, the United Nations demanded that the responsible members of Al Qaeda be turned over to the UN for trial. The Taliban refused, and the United Nations voted for an invasion of the country to seize the Al Qaeda leaders and, if necessary, overthrow the Taliban.

Afghanistan has always been a difficult country to subdue. The British learned that the hard way in the 19th century, when two successive invasions were beaten off by the local fighters. The Soviet Union learned the same lesson when resistance fighters defeated them in the 1980s.

Without a standing force of its own, the United Nations again turned to NATO, as it had when dealing with the former Yugoslavia, to provide military assistance. NATO agreed and, led by the U.S., began an assault on Afghanistan on October 7. Soon NATO had driven out the Taliban and was in control of the majority of the country. The most dangerous area was in the south, around the city of Kandahar. Assigned to bring the region under control, Canadian troops faced a difficult task.

In 2006 Taliban forces in Kandahar province were concentrated in Panjwaii, 30 kilometres west of Kandahar City. The insurgents were resisting efforts by the national government in Kabul to bring the region, located in the Arghandab River Valley, under legal control. In the summer of 2006 during the Battle of Panjwaii, NATO forces drove the Taliban out. But once NATO left the region, the insurgents quickly returned.

Determined to take control in the Panjwaii District, NATO developed Operation Medusa. Scheduled to start September 2, 2006, the plan called for Canadian troops to lead an attack supported by the

International Security Assistance Force (ISAF) and
the Afghan National Army. Troops from the 1st Battalion, the Royal Canadian Regiment battle group,
were supported by U.S. Army forces, Dutch and
Danish soldiers, and hundreds of Afghan Army
regulars. The region had been the scene of intense
fighting throughout the Battle of Panjwaii, with four
members of Task Force Orion, Canada's battalion-size
contribution to Afghanistan, killed on August 3. The
goal of Operation Medusa was to capture a series of
villages called Pashmul.

Always conscious of civilian casualties, the Canadians' first act was to notify everyone living in the
Panjwaii District to leave the area. Addressing the
media, Canadian officers warned both the citizens
and insurgents that an attack was eminent. Soon,
only the insurgents remained to face the combined
forces of NATO.

As dawn broke on September 2, Echo Battery of
the 2nd Regiment Royal Canadian Horse Artillery
was in place 10 kilometres north of the actual battlefield. The start of the battle was signalled by the roar
of heavy artillery pounding the enemy positions—
just as in World War I. Firing hundreds of rounds of
155-mm high-explosive shells from M777 howitzers,
the regiment hammered the suspected locations of
the insurgents.

In addition to the artillery, the Netherlands and
the United Kingdom used their Apache attack helicopters to aim rockets and 30-mm cannon fire on

targets as directed by observers on the ground. Above the helicopters, Harrier and F-16 fighter aircraft crisscrossed the sky delivering 500-pound bombs to other targets. And above them all at 4500 metres, U.S. Air Force B-1B bombers added their precision-guided weapons to the carnage on the ground. Soon, 200 Taliban fighters were dead and 80 surrendered.

As the bombing and strafing continued, NATO troops moved in from the north and south to seal off the area and trap the Taliban in an ever-tightening noose. Yet, despite the various roadblocks that barricaded all the roads in and out of the Panjwaii area, as many as 180 Taliban fighters slipped through the Allied lines—out of the fight but able to return another day.

With the Taliban in apparent retreat and the air campaign continuing, NATO commanders ordered the Canadians into the fray three full days ahead of the schedule. Canadian confidence was high. They knew the area well, having often patrolled its villages and grape and pomegranate fields in the past. Expectations were the Canadians would find little or no resistance.

The Royal Canadian Rifles (RCRs) were given the task of establishing NATO control on the ground. Charles Company (C Company), commanded by Major Matthew Sprague, led the attack. Major Mike Wright and Alpha Company (A Company) waited in the south, while on Highway 1, Major Geoff Abthorpe and Bravo Company (B Company) provided a screen in the north. Assisting the RCRs were engineers from the 23 Field Squadron, 2 Combat Engineer Regiment. The engineers would help the RCRs blast though any barrier that prevented the attackers from gaining their objectives.

On September 3 the Canadians moved out. C Company, leading the way, crossed the Arghandab River. As the attack force neared a white schoolhouse that had been the scene of numerous actions in the past, a flare arched through the sky—a signal to the dug-in defenders to ambush the force. The Canadians knew instantly that they were in trouble.

Almost immediately 7 Platoon's well-liked Warrant Officer Rick Nolan, sitting in the passenger seat of an armoured G-Wagon, was killed by a rocket-propelled grenade (RPG). A medic and Afghan interpreter sitting in the back seat were caught in the blast from the explosive rocket and badly wounded. Corporal Sean Teal pushed open the driver's door of the destroyed vehicle and braved a hail of enemy fire to seek medical assistance.

Things were no better for the armoured vehicle whose call sign was Echo 3-2. Struck by a round from an 82-mm recoilless rifle, the vehicle was destroyed and most of the men inside were wounded. Engineering Sergeant Shane Stachnik never had a chance. Riding in the air-sentry hatch of Echo 3-2, he was killed immediately when the shell struck.

It was now clear that the Canadians were in the midst of a full-out ambush. As the Canadians tried desperately to return fire, the enemy pressed in on three sides. Everything from AK-47 rifle bullets to RPGs was tearing at the Canadians. The situation quickly turned from bad to desperate.

Radios crackled with frantic calls for both medical aid and help holding back the enemy. Adam Day, writing about the battle, reported that: "Time got all messed up. It went too fast or it went too slow; hours seemed like minutes and some seconds took forever." Soldiers dragged wounded comrades to cover, tried to fire at the enemy, and deliver first aid—all at the same time.

Call sign 3-1 Bravo, an armoured personnel carrier, was quickly loaded with dead and wounded. The driver reversed away from the immediate danger at high speed but crashed backwards into a ditch. Its weak underbelly exposed, the carrier was hit by RPGs and was destroyed.

Desperate to get his men some relief, Major Sprague continually called in artillery strikes and air support. Under direct enemy fire himself, Sprague did all he could to keep the pressure on the well dug-in and fortified enemy. But his best efforts were not enough.

Private William Jonathan James Cushley was hit by heavy enemy fire and succumbed. Beside him, Frank Mellish, 8 Platoon's Warrant Officer, died trying to find a wounded friend in the chaos. The firing continued for hours, further devastating the ranks of the Canadians. Officers and men alike were hit, some more than once.

When a 1000-pound bomb from a friendly aircraft crashed through the Canadians and landed just in front of them without exploding, everyone knew they had used up all of their luck. Sprague received a radio call from Captain Derek Wessan. "We've gotta get the fuck out of here," he said. "And then we've gotta blow this place up." C Company withdrew with heavy losses. Of the 50 Canadians ambushed by the Taliban on September 2, four were killed and 10 wounded.

For the soldiers of Bravo Company, who could only listen to the battle raging in the south and knew that their comrades were in trouble, sitting and waiting was excruciating. "We had sort of felt left out from the start," explained Corporal Mike Blois, of 1 Section, 4 Platoon, B Company. "We knew from the radio what was going on, and we knew the PPCLI guys in Alpha would jump in to help, but these were guys from our regiment."

As if the ambush losses were not bad enough, two days later a U.S. Air Force A-10 Thunderbolt aircraft mistook C Company for enemy troops and hit the Canadians hard. Corporal Jason Plumley, attached to 23 Field Squadron, said: "I had been off to the side and heard the (A-10) sound. I hit the ground, and when I got up I saw all the [injured] laying there."

Private Mark Graham lay dead, and 30 others, including Major Sprague, were wounded. In less than 48 hours, Charles Company no longer existed as a fighting force.

With C Company out of the battle, NATO's attention switched from the south to the north of Panjwaii District. Recognizing that the enemy was in no mood to surrender, NATO began an intense artillery and air bombardment that ultimately killed another 51 Taliban.

Holding the line at Highway 1, Bravo Company was part of a force designed to trap what NATO estimated was a force of 700 Taliban fighters in the region. It was quiet—most of the time they engaged only stragglers near their positions—but not safe. On September 5, men from B Company came under enemy mortar fire as they were loading water and rations into their Light Armoured Vehicle. The Taliban, patiently waiting for the Canadians to drop their guard, wounded five.

Finally on September 6, B Company drove through the tree line dividing the Canadians from the enemy. This time the Canadians would not be surprised. Working forward methodically, the Canadians gained their objectives one by one. "It was almost like running a Recce Course," said Corporal Don Leblanc of RCR's Reconnaissance Platoon. "The difference is that we had all the assets we could ask for and more. We hadn't done much basic recce work in the work-up training, but our initial training kicked in and we went back to basics."

"We went from nothing to a three-hour firefight," said Corporal Blois. "It was strange, not what I expected. It was really intense but not scary." Blois described the enemy fire as similar to camera flashes. "I know a lot of guys think that they train and will never fight but I always figured that the Army trained for war and eventually I would be there."

The Canadians then settled into what could be described as a routine. With artillery and air support leading the way, and supported by a company of the U.S. 10th (Mountain) Division plus Afghan Army troops, the Canadians were soon clearing the region house by house and field by field.

After a brief calm, fighting erupted again on September 8 and continued into the next day. Forty Taliban fighters and one American were killed as the ISAF started occupying areas of both the Panjwaii and Zhari districts. Three Taliban positions, a bomb-making factory and an arms cache were also destroyed by ground troops.

The Taliban weren't ready to concede. On September 9, 94 militants were killed while facing the ISAF troops. Another 92 were killed the following day when the militants staged a counterattack against NATO forces. As NATO troops slowly probed forward during the next four days, it became clear that even as the Canadians and their allies solidified their hold on the area, the Taliban had slipped away. As the soldiers checked each house, compound and farm building, they found evidence that the Taliban had indeed been ready to fight, and they had booby trapped many of the buildings as they left.

On the morning of September 14, NATO troops moved into Pashmula. According to reports carried by CanWest News, the troops found, "50 kilograms of nitrogen, dozens of batteries, rocket-propelled grenades, ammunition, tunnels and bunkers." The same CanWest News story quoted Bravo Company's Major Geoff Abthorpe, "Caution is the name of the game today. Slow is smooth, and smooth is fast."

Canadian soldiers taking part in house-to-house searches were concerned that the escaping Taliban would simply return to attack them another day. That concern increased to anxiety when an Afghan interpreter attached to the Canadians reported hearing radio traffic from the Taliban indicating that, in fact, they had not withdrawn but were digging in to continue the fight.

The Canadians need not have worried about facing the enemy again—at least not in this battle. Intelligence reports later confirmed that 400 Taliban fighters had retreated into Farah province, burning a district headquarters and a local clinic as they retreated. On September 17, Operation Medusa was over. NATO had driven the Taliban from the Kandahar City region and from the Panjwaii and Zhari districts of Kandahar province.

For Canada, Operation Medusa was costly. Five Canadians died during major combat operations, another five in roadside bombings and two in a mortar attack during reconstruction efforts after the battle ended. In addition to the 12 Canadians, 12 British and one American soldier paid the ultimate price while trying to bring security to a very troubled country.

Notes on Sources

General

Beacock Fryer, Mary. *Battlefields of Canada*. Toronto: Dundurn Press, 1986.

Beacock Fryer, Mary. *More Battlefields of Canada*. Toronto: Dundurn Press, 1993.

Bishop, Arthur. *True Canadian Heroes on the Battlefield*. Toronto: Key Porter Books, 2004.

Bishop, Arthur. *True Canadian Battles that Forged Our Nation*. Toronto: Key Porter Books, 2008.

Granatstein, J.L. *Canada's Army: Waging War and Keeping the Peace*. Toronto: University of Toronto Press, 2002.

Horn, Bernd (editor) *Forging a Nation: Perspectives on the Canadian Military Experience*. St. Catherines: Vanwell Publishing, Ltd., 2002.

Humphreys, Edward. *Great Canadian Battles: Heroism and Courage Through the Years*. London: Arcurus Publishing Limited, 2008.

Marteinson, John. *We Stand on Guard: An Illustrated History of the Canadian Army*. Montreal: Ovale Publications, 1992.

Paterson, T.W. *Canadian Battles & Massacres*. Langley, BC: Stagecoach Publishing Company Ltd., 1977.

The Beginnings of Canada

Schwartz, Seymour I. *The French and Indian War 1754–1763: The Imperial Struggle for North America.* New York: Simon & Schuster, 1994.

War of 1812

Dale, Ronald. *The Invasion of Canada.* Toronto: James Lorimer and Company, 2001.

Fitzgibbon, Mary Agnes. *A Veteran of 1812.* Toronto: William Briggs, 1894.

Gray, William. *Soldiers of the King: The Upper Canadian Militia 1812–1815.* Erin: Stoddard, 1995.

Rebellion of 1837

Tiffany, Orrin Edward. *The Canadian Rebellion of 1837–38.* Toronto: Coles Publishing Company Ltd., 1980.

Fenian Raids

Gagnan, David. *The Denison Family of Toronto: 1792–1925.* Toronto: University of Toronto Press, 1973.

Riel Rebellion

Asfar, Dan and Tim Chodan. *Louis Riel.* Edmonton: Folklore Publishing, 2003.

Asfar, Dan and Tim Chodan. *Gabriel Dumont: War Leader of the Métis.* Edmonton: Folklore Publishing, 2003.

Beal, Bob and Rod Macleod. *Prairie Fire: The 1885 Northwest Rebellion.* Edmonton: Hurtig Publishers, 1984.

Brown, Wayne E. *Steele's Scouts: Samuel Benefield Steele and the North-West Rebellion.* Surrey, BC: Heritage House Publishing Company Ltd. 2001.

Hollihan, Tony. *Kootenai Brown.* Edmonton: Folklore Publishing, 2001.

MacEwan, Grant. *Colonel James Walker: Man of the Western Frontier.* Saskatoon: Western Producer Prairie Books, 1989.

Boer War

Evans, W. Sanford. *The Canadian Contingents.* Toronto: The Publishers Syndicate, Ltd. 1901.

Sibbald, Raymond. *The Boer War.* Gloucestershire: Bramley Books, 1997.

World War I

Baker, David. *William Avery "Billy" Bishop: The Man and the Aircraft He Flew.* London: Outline Press, 1990

Beatty, David Pierce. *The Vimy Pilgrimage, July 1936.* Amherst, Nova Scotia: Acadian Printing, 1987.

Berton, Pierre. *Vimy.* Toronto: Anchor Canada, 2001.

Bishop, (Lieutenant Colonel) William. *Winged Warfare: the Greatest Canadian Fighter Pilot Tells his Own Story.* Toronto: Totem Books, 1976.

Dancocks, Daniel. *Legacy of Valour: The Canadians at Passchendaele.* Edmonton: Hurtig Publishers, 1986.

Dobson, Christopher and John Miller. *The Day They Almost Bombed Moscow: The Allied War in Russia 1918–1920.* New York: Atheneum, 1986.

Evans, Martin Marix. *Battles of World War I.* London: Arcturus Publishing Ltd., 2008.

Gudmundson, Bruce I. *Stormtroop Tactics: Innovation in the German Army, 1914–1918.* New York: Praeger, 1989.

Macksey, Kenneth (Major). *The Shadow of Vimy Ridge.* Toronto: Ryerson Press, 1965.

Morton, Desmond and J.L. Granatstein. *Marching to Armageddon: Canadians and the Great War 1914–1919.* Toronto: Lester & Orpen Dennys Limited, 1989.

Mills, Stephen. *Task of Gratitude: Canadian Battlefields of the Great War.* Winnipeg, Bunker to Bunker Books, 1997.

Platt, Frank. *Great Battles of World War I: In The Air.* New
    York: Weathervane Books, 1966.
Morley, James William. *The Japanese Thrust into Siberia,
    1918.* New York: Columbia University Press, 1957.
Swettenham, John. *Allied Intervention in Russia, 1918–1919:
    and the part played by Canada.* London: George Allen &
    Unwin Ltd., 1967.

World War II

Bishop, Arthur. *The Splendid Hundred: The True Story of
    Canadians who Flew in The Greatest Air Battle of World
    War II.* Toronto: McGraw-Hill Ryerson, 1994.
Brewster, Hugh. *On Juno Beach: Canada's D-Day Heroes.*
    Markham, Ont: Scholastic, 2004.
Boutilier, James. *RCN In Retrospect: 1910–1968.* Vancouver:
    University of British Columbia, 1982.
Fraser, Doug. *Postwar Casualty: Canada's Merchant Navy.*
    Nova Scotia: Pottersfield Press, 1997.
Gray, Larry. *Canadians in the Battle of the Atlantic.*
    Edmonton: Folklore Publishing, 2007.
Gray, Larry. *Canada's World War II Aces: Heroic Pilots and
    Gunners of the Wartime Skies.* Edmonton: Folklore Pub-
    lishing, 2006.
Benedict, Michael. *On the Battlefields: Two World Wars that
    Shaped a Nation.* London: Penguin Books, 2002.
Whitaker, (Brigadier General) Denis. *Dieppe: Tragedy to
    Triumph.* Whitby: McGraw Hill, 1992.
Villa, Brian Loring. *Unauthorized Action: Mountbatten and
    the Dieppe Raid.* Toronto: Oxford University Press,
    1990.

Korean War

Barris, Ted. *Deadlock in Korea: Canadians at War, 1950–
    1953.* Toronto: Macmillan Canada, 1999.

Bercuson, David J. *Blood on the Hills: The Canadian Army in the Korean War.* Toronto: University of Toronto Press, 2002.

McKeown, Michael (Captain). *Kapyong Remembered: Anecdotes from Korea.* Unknown, 1976.

Thomas, Nigel. *The Korean War 1950–1953.* Oxford: Osprey Publishing, 1986.

Peacekeeping

Blatchford, Christie. *Fifteen Days.* Toronto: Anchor, 2008.

Gorst, Anthony and Lewis Johnman. *The Suez Crisis.* London: Routledge, 1997.

MacKenzie, (Major General) Lewis. *Peacekeeper: The Road to Sarajevo.* Toronto: Douglas & McIntyre, 1993.

Melady, John. *Pearson's Prize: Canada and the Suez Crisis.* Toronto: The Dundurn Group, 2006.

Off, Carol. *The Ghosts of Medak Pocket.* Toronto: Random House, 2004.

Off, Carol. *The Lion, The Fox and the Eagle.* Toronto: Random House, 2000.

Pigott, Peter. *Canada in Afghanistan: The War So Far.* Toronto: Dundurn Press, 2007.

Robertson, Terrence. *Crisis: The Inside Story of the Suez Conspiracy.* Toronto: McClelland and Stewart Limited, 1964.

Staples, Michael Anthony. *Combat Ready: Travelling with Canada's Peacekeepers in the Former Yugoslavia.* Fredericton: Unipress Limited, 2000.

Taylor, Scott and Brian Nolan. *Tested Mettle: Canada's Peacekeepers at War.* Ottawa: Esprit de Corps Books, 1998.

Norman Leach

Norman Leach is a historian, freelance writer and professional speaker from Calgary, Alberta. He graduated with a degree in Strategic Studies from the University of Manitoba, and now gives presentations around the world on Canadian military history.

Norman's writing has won him two Crystal Awards from the University of Lethbridge, and he has been awarded both the Canadian 125 and Alberta Centennial Medals. He has also been named an honourary peacekeeper by the Canadian Armed Forces. Most recently, he served as historical advisor on the Paul Gross film Passchendaele.

Norman says he is not interested in writing the great tomes about which battalion moved up when. He is fascinated by the true stories of the officers and soldiers who have been lost to time. Their lives, their sacrifices and their successes and failures are Norman's true work. This is his second book for Folklore Publishing; his first was *Canadian Peacekeepers*.